KAAM

Don't st-p
growing

ALL YOU WANT

All You Want

Victor Armando Martinez

Printed in the United States of America

First Printing: May 2018

ISBN-13: 978-1718601413

Pastors Victor and Daysi Martinez

Pastor Victor is the founder and Lead Pastor of New Generation Church, a.k.a. SoyNGChurch. Pastor Daysi currently serves as Assistant Pastor at NGC.

ALL YOU WANT

"What are

Your

Desires"

About the Author

Reverend Victor Armando Martinez is the founder and Lead Pastor of New Generation Church, a.k.a. SoyNGChurch.

Establishing NGC in 2013, Rev. Victor is a motivational speaker and persuasive preacher who speaks at fundraising events, conferences, on television, and radio. He serves as the current Vice-Chairman at the Northside Residential Redevelopment Council in North Minneapolis.

He is the only child born to Bertha Martinez and Armando Barajas and was raised solely by his mother along with five of his siblings. He believes in preaching and teaching the word of God, and more importantly, he believes that we must **"LIVE"** the Word in all areas of our lives.

Victor Martinez is a no-nonsense, open and transparent man of God. His high level of integrity, honesty, discipline and strong application of personal mentoring discipleship has earned him immense respect and an enviable reputation wherever he finds himself.

Prior to his calling as a minister, he served as a Youth Pastor for over 11 years.

Pastor Victor is a pace-setter and a catalyst for change and he has devoted all of his life to bettering the lives of everyone around him through spiritual and personal mentorship.

Pastor Victor attended Bethel University and is currently furthering his education at the Assemblies of God, Minnesota School of Ministry—this is in line with his belief that continued education is a key to advancing the Kingdom of God.

Pastor Victor Martinez has been married to Pastor Daysi Martinez for six years, having been joined in holy matrimony on the **7th of May, 2012**.

Pastor Daysi currently serves as Assistant Pastor at NGC. She has earned a certificate of ministry from the Assemblies of God and is also pursuing further education at the Minnesota School of Ministry. She has preached and taught at conferences and has been on the radio and television spreading the good news of the gospel.

Pastors Victor and Daysi Martinez live in Minneapolis, MN and are blessed with three beautiful children: two daughters, Priscilla and Victoria; and a son, Valentin.

ALL YOU WANT

Table of Contents

Growing up with no father, bad examples and finding the

Perfect Father

My earliest childhood memories are of me playing in front of my Grandma's house. Sitting next to a tree, I would play with plastic cars which I received as Christmas gifts

~|~

~|~

~|~

~|~

I want to illustrate Gods framework as easy and as simple as possible. In order to be in a position to ask God for your desires and wants, you have to work together all the key parts. Applying one without the other will not work but will cause confusion and unnecessary frustration

~|~

The men and women of God were often very prosperous

~|~

Dedication

I dedicate this book to **my Lord and Saviour, Jesus Christ**, because in Him I have found what I have always been looking for:

Peace that surpasses all understanding, Joy unspeakable and everything else that cannot be bought with money. Words cannot express how excited and thankful I am for the things You have given- and shown me.

To my wife, who has collaborated and inspired me to write this book, I say: *"Thank you for loving me even when I did not deserve it."*

To my children: *"Because of you, I have seen God's love and promises fulfilled in my life."*

Finally, I dedicate this book to each of those **people who have provided or displayed bad examples during my childhood years**. *All of you contributed to the development of my character and personal growth. Some of you had evil intentions, but God, who is the Perfector and Finisher of my Faith, has worked it all together for good.*

ALL YOU WANT

Preface

All around me I have seen people make the same mistakes over and over; mistakes that have left hearts broken and families divided; mistakes that leave people empty, sad and unfulfilled, always looking for love, direction and purpose in all the wrong places.

We no longer dream and hope for greater things as we did when we were children. The sky used to be our limit and the world was our playground to enjoy. What happened to us? When did it go wrong?

We made mistakes and wrong decisions, sometimes one after another; got some bumps and bruises in the process... and we began to settle for less.

Simply based on the fact that he does not physically beat her, a young girl settles for a man that doesn't respect her, that verbally abuses her and constantly degrades her every time he gets angry.

We "**settle for less**" with our finances; our prayers become prayers of low expectation, such as: "*God just help me pay my bills*", instead of, "*Lord teach me to prosper. Show me how to have more than enough.*"

We "**settle for less**" with our families, saying: "*As long as my kids have food in their bellies and a roof over their heads they'll be fine.*" We don't want to hear what God expects from us as parents; He not only wants our children to survive, He wants them to thrive in everything they do… especially in their relationship with Him.

Do not be offended; the Bible tells us that the truth will make us free. God wants more for us and our families.

What if I told you that the God Who created the Universe loves you? That he loves you so very much that he actually wants to give you the desires and wishes of your heart? He doesn't care what you have done, or where you have been, or what you have been through; he doesn't care where you have started your life at.

When I first heard this particular statement, I made a conscious and bold decision to investigate and find out if it was true… because if it were, I knew it would have the power to change people's lives forever.

In this book I will tell you how God gave me the desires of my heart, how he actualized my dreams and made

4

them a reality and more importantly, I will tell you how he can give you all you want!

Truth is, we are the ones that are complicated... not God. We complicate things for ourselves, and then we blame everybody but ourselves for the consequences.

I will show you in this book how to un-complicate things and give you the framework that God gave humankind. Living by this "*framework*", I got my dream-girl who was my first kiss, my first everything.

I will also show you how God brought all my other dreams to pass; even dreams that I was too scared to speak out; dreams that seemed impossible.

Although it involved a great amount of patience and a lot of faith, it turned out to be more than worth it. I will share with you stories of other people who dared to believe- and trust God for the desires of their hearts!

I want to thank my wife, **Daysi Martinez**, for sharing a snapshot of her life for all to see. She shares with us her perspective of how God gave her the desires of her heart.

I would also like to thank **Josh Clintwood** for his personal story of how he met the love of his life, *Morgan*. Thank you, *Josh*, for your transparency.

Many times, people live with damaged lives; they don't know who they are anymore or how to dream again; they don't know how to ask for help, or for what they want or need...

The great news is that God understands our brokenness. He is in there with us. He sees past the pain and confusion that is our lives. The only thing that God asks for during this process, is an honest and hungry heart, longing for God to move in our circumstances.

I like to say: "*Give Him room to operate, and He will not disappoint.*" So many people need to hear that there is hope and that things can turn around. I guarantee that God really **CAN** give you the desires of your heart! And that He **WANTS** to…

Reflection

Questions for this Section

Answer the following questions taken from this section, and focus your mind

Write down your answers and thoughts

1. What are some things you used to dream of having or becoming when you were a child?

_____

_____

_____

_____

_____

_____

_____

_____

_____

_____

_____

_____

_____

_____

_____

_____

_____

2. What are some dreams and goals you have now?

_____

_____

_____

_____

_____

_____

_____

_____

_____

_____

_____

_____

_____

_____

_____

_____

_____

_____

_____

Chapter 1

No One to Teach, No One to Lead - Ages 0-7 - Growing up with no father, bad examples and finding the perfect Father

My earliest childhood memories are of me playing in front of my Grandma's house. Sitting next to a tree, I would play with plastic cars which I received as Christmas gifts.

I remember that I played by myself; I was a loner.

9

The only Father Figures that I had during the first 7 years of my life were Uncles on my mom's side who liked to get drunk and then fight. I did have one uncle who did not drink and who was super nice though. My **Tio Gordo** was very big (at least from my perspective at the time).

I was scared of being around him all by myself. My most vivid memory of him is the fact that he was mentally disabled and that he was inflicted by frequent seizures.

I also had a number of cousins who, for some reason, seemed to be very rugged. I remember them being disobedient to our Grandmother.

I usually tell people who ask me where I'm from that I was made in Mexico and born in Escondido, California. When I was about 1 year old, my mom took me to live with my grandmother in Mexico for about 2 years.

Then my mom came back to my grandmother and brought me back to California to live with her.

My stay with my mother did not last long; soon after, I was taken back to live with my Grandmother in Mexico. This time, my younger brother Joel and my older sister Lucy came along.

My siblings and I were eventually brought back to the States some time later when I was about 4 years old. I remember that my mom worked all the time and never really had time for us. She often had mental breakdowns, the reason for which I never completely understood.

I remember telling my younger sibling, on one specific occasion while my mother was sobbing, that our mom was crazy. I never saw my mom as "**Mom**"; to me, she was just a regular person.

We lived below the poverty line and had very little; we had just enough to get by and survive; but compared to how I lived in Mexico, I found that all my needs were well met.

I remember attending churches because of the help they could give us: sometimes it was food and other times clothes or Christmas gifts. These were my first experiences of "**Church**". I experienced churches as a refuge; a safe place to find peace and stability; a place to run into whenever I was in need and which would always provide for me.

My first experience with love and/or affection, as far as I can remember, was with a young white woman whom I had a crush on. She would often make brownies for my brother and I and invite us to her home to eat them.

My second experience was with my first school teacher who used to come to my house to visit. I remember that she'd often hug me and treat me with much love and affection. I cannot remember my mother ever doing this; she rarely showed us love and affection.

Life started changing for us when my eldest brother, Jorge, began to attend church. A bus would pick us up at our apartment every Sunday morning. We had

Sunday school class and then we would sing songs and listen to Bible stories.

I remember getting treats and participating in games, one of which involved sitting still: staying still the longest as a soldier would earn the winner a prize... I never used to win any of those games, though.

I do not recall any memories of an adult that ever took the time and made the effort to get to know me or even talk to me... not even engaging in small talk... I was like a sponge, hollow inside, deficient and lacking emotions, but eagerly waiting for someone to lead and teach me about life and love, ready to soak up whatever they had to teach.

With time, I began to understand the teachings in Sunday school; God began to become real to me, and I felt within my spirit that He did not want us to do bad things; that we made Him really sad when we did those bad things.

Then one day, out of the blue, our mom told us that we were moving to Minnesota. We only heard about the move on that particular day...

To me, 'Life' as a kid was not a pleasant experience. While most kids had experiences of their fathers taking them out and buying them toys, gifts and fancy treats, my memories consisted of Uncles being drunk and fighting; while my peers had their mothers showering them with love and affection, providing for their everyday needs, my mother didn't provide for my emotional needs. She was always busy and didn't have time for my siblings and I. To me, it seemed that she couldn't care less about our development, obviously thinking that her duty as a mother ended at providing us with a daily meal.

The fact that my first experience with love was at the hands of a stranger was pitiful and not what it was supposed to be at all. The family is the smallest unit of the community that is bound by bonds of love and affection; it is where a child is supposed to first learn- and experience these values.

To say the very least, in all honesty, I had a family that lacked the basics that should be provided by the family unit; values such as: love, affection, friendship and familiarity. There was no hand to guide me through the beginnings of my life and teach me these essential core values and emotions. This was the kind of childhood that formed the foundation of my mental, physical and spiritual development.

This chapter highlights the fact that I was deprived of love and affection; that I have never experienced the love of a father, nor the love of a mother. Somewhere, somehow, a void was left in me; a lack of things that are taken for granted by most; a lack of parental presence and guidance while growing up; that love and nurturing that parents should provide to their children from Day 1 of their existence.

I was deprived of all these, and my reason for mentioning this is that I want you to take a lesson from this, my experience; that no matter what kind of childhood you had, no matter how negative the beginning of our life was, no matter how messed up or perfect it was, it does not matter. It does not disqualify you from getting all that you desire from God, and more.

God does not discriminate, nor does He snub; in fact, He does the exact opposite of that: He embraces.

So, learn from this chapter that no matter what kind of childhood you had, he is still ready to listen to you and give you your heart's desires and wishes. All that you want...

Reflection

Questions for Chapter 1

Answer the following questions taken from this section, and focus your mind

Write down your answers and thoughts

1. What are some of your earliest memories as a child?

_____

_____

_____

_____

_____

_____

_____

_____

_____

_____

_____

2. What are some of your earliest memories of love and affection?

_____

_____

_____

_____

_____

_____

_____

_____

_____

_____

_____

_____

3. (for some) Do you think your parents' lack of love had something to do with how they were raised, why or why not?

_____

_____

_____

_____

_____

_____

_____

_____

_____

_____

4. Name a few that you things you wish you had while growing up?

_____

_____

_____

_____

_____

_____

_____

_____

ALL YOU WANT

Chapter 2

Too Ignorant To Know Anything about Life - Ages 8-13

Moving to Minnesota marked quite a huge shift in my life; it was a change in perspective and experience.

Our family went from going out all the time, such as going to the beach, visiting flea markets, taking random walks, to staying indoors most of the time. Winter in MN does that to a person.

I remember growing up to be a chubby pale looking kid who did not get enough exercise and ate too many unhealthy meals. I started school in Shakopee, Minnesota, continuing my loner lifestyle from where I left off in California.

I remember staying by myself, keeping away from other kids. Taking this as an excuse, they often did bad things; however, the truth was that I was scared because of my inability to connect with others.

Looking back now, as an adult, I realize that this inability to connect with people stemmed from the fact that I had a very low self-esteem; I lacked self-confidence, and that was the reason why I stayed away from others.

I was not street-smart at all. I let people walk all over me and push me around. I could not and did not defend myself from their bullying... I was a coward. I did not tell anyone about my experiences under the abusive hands of the bullies for fear of their retaliation.

I also did not want to be perceived as "weak" by my family. I would shut down and keep to myself in conflict situations. I became adept at internalizing. I literally got stuck and couldn't move when I was being bullied because I was terrified.

I would keep quiet whenever I came across an act of injustice, because I was too scared to speak out. I felt that my thoughts and beliefs did not matter and would not really change anything; that I did not really matter in the grand scheme of things; how wrong I was!

I have memories of times when I drank from the school fountain and some of the kids would make fun of me and flung really unflattering, cruel and condescending remarks at me, such as: "Don't drink up the whole ocean", meaning that I had an abyss in me; that I was some sort of monster from a comic book.

I would immediately go to the bathroom and cry my eyes out, feeling sorry for myself; I used to feel sorry for myself a lot. Self-pity was the only way I could comfort and console myself, so I wallowed in it... and I did it well. I was an outcast.

I also had another problem: I couldn't approach girls that I liked and talk to them--. The fear was so real, I could touch it; I did not know how to talk to them, and was always nervous, timid and shy around them.

I remember having this really huge crush on a girl that was at my sister's "**quinceanera**" once. I was so nervous that I could not bring myself to utter a word to her; I couldn't think up even one word to say to her.

The Pastor's wife was in attendance and noticed my timidity; she then told me: "*Just go over there and talk to her.*"

I then walked over to the girl to try and strike up a conversation with her. My legs felt like lead and they became heavier with each step I took towards her; I actually made it to where she was but guess what: I couldn't say one word! My tongue also felt like lead and I couldn't get it to move in speech.

High School...

When I started high school, I lost a lot of weight and gained a lot of muscle. I thought I was turning a new page in my life, leaving behind all the unpleasant ways, breaking out of my cocoon like a butterfly. I was finally going to shed my fears and childish limitations; I was going to get over my nervousness and timidity. I even decided to start using my real first name, Victor. Formerly, I used my middle name, Armando. To me, using my first name, Victor, reflected power and confidence. This would be a symbol of my new-found life; of my new-found identity as a new and stronger person. However, none of that "**resolution stuff**" worked; neither did the constant words of encouragement that I spoke to myself, or the change of name or anything else I tried. Nothing worked to rebuild and restore my destroyed self-esteem and self-confidence.

Girls would start taking notice of me, maybe even smile at me...

A smile from a girl was something that was considered everywhere as a sign of interest and encouragement to the guy... but I always thought to myself: "*They don't really like me, they're just having their laughs and making fun of me.*"

I was still not free of my mental shackles; Mentally, I was still stuck in my childhood while trying to make a show of confidence externally.

On one occasion, a friend of mine whom I played football with, told me that one of his female friends, Jacqui, liked me.

I would walk by her locker day after day, our eyes meeting; each time she would lower her gaze shyly.

It crossed my mind several times to approach her and talk to her; to at least strike up a conversation with her and see if we could be friends; but I would say to myself: *"She doesn't really like me; it's just a joke on me."*

This was my way of *"chickening out."* Obviously, I was still not over my timidity and nervousness. I always pulled out instead of summoning the courage to talk to her.

On another occasion, one of my beautiful female friends was hitting on me for a while. She would meet me by my locker whenever she could, asking me to walk her to class and restrooms. She would smile at me, saying *"thank you"* as she walked into class. Yet I kept telling myself that she does not like me and was just being friendly and nice.

"Nobody would like me. I'm fat and ugly," I would say to myself, inadvertently knocking myself down even more each time.

"I don't know anything about life," I would tell God. *"Please help me."*

I often felt unconnected and out of touch with life. I felt like I was differed from other people; like they did not understand me and I did not understand them; as if I was an alien and not really a part of or from this world.

I remember another experience with a girl from church; it was quite obvious that she liked me.

My brothers, sister and church friends would say to me, "**go talk to her, she likes you.**" They would encourage me and try to get me to break out of my comfort zone; to at least try and see what things would be like.

The opportunity came at last... she was at my house, visiting.

I approached her, after finally summoning enough courage to talk to her, and messed up yet again:

"**Why do you like me?**" I asked.

That must have been the most stupid and tactless first statement from a guy in my position to a girl in hers.

Her reply to my question: "**Only as a friend.**"

Imagine what effect that had on me! Instead of helping me achieve some form of satisfaction and a level of confidence, it ended up doing the exact opposite. It was devastating! I couldn't seem to get rid of my ever-present feeling of insecurity.

I began to hate myself; to feel a strong dislike for anything that had 'me' in it. I did not want to see my own picture. I would erase my face out of family portraits just so I would not see myself.

I began to struggle in school, in various aspects. I was not performing like I used to. Things went from bad to worse, literally. It was like living in a nightmare. I did not know much about God at the time as I didn't really have much experience related to Him, neither did I have a real big opportunity to connect with Him, but one thing I did know and was sure of from the little I had learned: God loved me. He cared about me deeply and he could help me and would do everything within His power to guard and protect me. I was convinced of this fact, and it was something I clung to during all of those hopelessly devastating times; those days when I felt gloomy and everything was dark around me.

Day after day, I asked God to take me out of the school I was attending at the time, and to send me to some other place. Anywhere would do.

I asked Him for a new start; a new beginning; a new atmosphere and climate that would let me thrive and fully express myself; a new place where I could live a great life, one that was better than this one I was living at the time.

I would cry and plead with Him to save me because I could not handle it anymore; I could not go on living with how my circumstances were anymore. And you know what? He heard my prayers and did exactly what I requested of Him.

Halfway through my sophomore year in high school, God moved me to the place that I least wanted to go to: **North Minneapolis**. North Minneapolis had a bad reputation. I would continue my high school education at **Patrick Henry High**, and everything would change.

This was my first experience in which God granting me the desires of my heart. I didn't understand it at the time, but God would turn it around for me.

At my current school, **Harding High, St Paul, MN**, I struggled in class. I would achieve only one 'A' in the first year and a half there, that was in Spanish class. I also struggled with temptation (**Harding** had a very relaxed dress code, and many of the ladies used to dress scandalously); and I struggled with confidence and a low self-image.

Little did I know that God would grant me my request at my new school; the school I didn't want to attend. By the time I began my senior year; I would get straight 'A's, was voted student body president, was voted runner-up for **Homecoming King**, lead the **Christian Youth Club** as President, represented my high school at the **State Student Council**, was elected to The **American Legion Boys' State Convention** and was no longer easily distracted by girls in mini shirt and low-cut shirts (**Henry** had a very strict dress code, which helped removed distractions).

The new setting helped me to gain confidence and develop into the person I had always hoped for; God had given me exactly what I needed and wanted!

Having read this chapter, you will gather that I've had some "**personal demons**" to fight, such as a low self-esteem, low self-confidence and people (mostly at school) not seeing much good in me, always taunting me, making a joke of me and bullying me. I did not see any good in myself, either. I did have friends, yet I felt alienated; like I was not good enough.

I couldn't hold down a normal conversation without being afraid of *'messing things up'*; I couldn't approach girls without being nervous and timid; I had a really low opinion of myself... but God does not care about that. He does not care how damaged you are; he does not care how rejected and unwanted you are or how you belittle yourself. God does not see that, nor will he reject you.

Instead, God will help you; he will work with what little is left of the "**real**" you and will work on you and help you overcome your challenges. He does not care what your opinion of yourself is or how badly you see yourself. In fact, often times the lesser you think about yourself, the more you allow Him to manifest Himself and work His miracle.

The Bible says that ***His strength is manifested in our weakness***. ***When we are weak, He is strong***.

Your opinion of yourself and other peoples' opinions of you do not matter to Him; do you consider yourself to be "**damaged goods?**" Take heart: ***God fixes damaged goods***; whether you consider yourself unworthy of being loved, he loves you nonetheless. What is difficult to you is easy to Him. No human can unscramble an egg… but God can.

27

Reflection

Questions for Chapter 2

Answer the following questions taken from this section, and focus your mind

Write down your answers and thoughts

1. (as a child) How did you handle conflict?

_____

_____

_____

_____

_____

_____

_____

_____

_____

_____

_____

_____

2. (as a child) How did you express your feelings and emotions to those around you?

_____

_____

_____

_____

_____

_____

_____

_____

_____

_____

3. How can God turn your childhood into a tool for your life?

_____

_____

_____

_____

_____

_____

_____

_____

_____

_____

_____

ALL YOU WANT

Chapter 3

The Start of Crazy Childlike Faith (Ages 14-16)

Avoiding painful regrets - The art of seeking biblical wisdom

The Bible relates a story about King Solomon; a story about as interesting and intriguing as the character of the man himself.

It tells of an angel that came to visit Solomon; this was after Solomon had done certain things that pleased the Lord God of Israel.

The angel told Solomon that he would grant Him one desire, one wish, anything he wanted the most in the world, and it would be granted.

See 2 Chronicles 1:7-11

"***Wow***", I said to myself. "***What a special, awesome gift!***"

My mind immediately began to race and consider all the possibilities; all the options he had and could choose from; everything that he could accomplish with his one, new, "**super power.**" Perhaps he would ask to destroy all his enemies... he was the King of Israel after all and Israel had many enemies troubling them.

Or he would ask to be the most powerful man alive; even more than any King that had ever lived. Or perhaps it would be wealth; riches upon riches, the type of which the world had never seen before... or perhaps he would ask to be immortal and never die, to be a King forever and retain his throne.

When I heard what he requested, I was taken aback because quite frankly, I couldn't understand it. It was far too simple in my childish opinion; the thing he had requested from God was... **Wisdom!** Wisdom to govern God's chosen people.

I said to myself,

"***Okay... that was cool, but what about the rest of the great, awesome stuff?***"

It was a little below all the others and incomparable to them; like having a choice between living in the

Buckingham Palace or a bungalow and choosing the bungalow... my limited understanding greatly hindered me from seeing the importance and Wisdom of his choice.

The next part of the story knocked me off my feet, leaving me amazed and in awe. The Angel told Him that since he did not ask for the power to destroy His enemies, or for riches, that he would have them all anyway; he was even going to get the things he had not asked for. In other words, he would be able to accomplish every other thing he needed, and even more, because of the new dose of Wisdom God gifted him with. He had not been narrow-minded or selfish. He had been wise and had chosen **Wisdom** as his gift from God.

This was an eye-opener to me.

It spoke and connected to me right away: if I asked God for **Wisdom like Solomon did**, I would be greatly blessed as well. It was a cheat; a way to accomplish a number of things in one shot; a way of killing multiple birds with one stone.

During this time, I had heard that the book of *Proverbs* was full of wise, Godly advice; advice written mainly by the wise King himself.

I began to study the book of *Proverbs* so that I could become wise myself and have all those other things that come with it.

I found a verse in Proverbs that says:

"Wisdom cries out on the street for someone to listen."

It was at that very moment that I realized that few people listen to God's advice about life, love and everything in-between; few people really cared for His Wisdom and lived their lives the way they wanted; few people commit themselves into His care and allow Him to take the reins of their life and direct them. Another verse in that particular book says:

"He who lacks Wisdom, he must ask, for God gives Wisdom abundantly."

That was it, the golden word I had been searching for, and I had found the secret. From then on, I chose to listen to God's word, live and tread in His laid down path and ask for Wisdom. In fact, every day for the next 3 years was filled with *"requesting Wisdom."* I begged and cried out for God to give me Wisdom, to bestow and improve my thinking faculty; I wanted to please Him; to abide by His rules.

Something began to happen as I soaked in the Word of God. My heart and mind began to see things differently. I began to improve and become a better person and to develop confidence in myself like I've never had before; the confidence that had eluded me for such a long time and which I had tried to build to no avail on my own strength.

Fear and nervousness began to flee from my life and became things of the past; my relationship with God exploded into an active and passionate one in which we engaged each other as God would speak to me through His word and I would communicate with Him through prayer.

I began to trust God more and more with the dawning of every single day. I realized how much God actually loved me. All those stories I had heard about His love for me suddenly took on new meaning, I had a deeper understanding of Him and His love for me. The fact that he cares about every issue in my life suddenly became quite glaring.

Because of this new-found confidence and Wisdom, I was able to accumulate all of those accolades in High School. I become influential in my own circle of friends. In fact, I not only had real confidence I began to reach out to other students that were outcast; students that nobody talked to. I befriended them and encouraged them. I had made a 180-degree turn into a new life. God was granting my desires one at a time.

The challenge

As my relationship with God grew, so did my confidence. I began to look for people who talked on different biblical issues so that I could learn from them, and in so doing, develop and improve my relationship with Him.

That year, a challenge was extended on a Christian radio station; the outcome of that challenge would be the beginning of something new in my life; the spark that lit the fire that would eventually result in a blaze and bring me to write this book 18 years later.

The challenge was: *"If you really trust God then ask God for what you really want; be specific."*

They made the case for men to ask God for the wife they really wanted; to be specific with your wants and desires. They read a verse in the bible that I didn't hear much about in Church or Bible studies:

"Delight yourself in the LORD, and he will give you the desires of your heart."

Psalm 37:4 (ESV)

I heard that the more specific you are with God, the more faith you put into action. God's kingdom runs on nothing but faith and the more faith you can channel into something, the more belief you have in His ability to accomplish something for your sake, the more likely it is for that particular thing to come to pass. If you put your trust in Him and walk in His way, he will definitely help you accomplish your heart's desires and give you whatever you want!

"For in it the righteousness of God is revealed from faith for faith, as it is written: the righteous shall live by faith."

Romans 1:17 (ESV)

As an analogy, picture a man who owns a car dealership containing every type and model of car that exists on this planet; from vintage 'Benz to the new electric cars on the block. Now picture that man having a son who will soon turn 18; picture him wanting to give his son a car for his birthday. Picture the man asking his son to make a choice of any type of car he wants.

Now, put yourself in the position of that son, and imagine what you would do in that situation...

I would assume that, based on your knowledge that your father has access to every type of car and that he loves you enough to grant anything you wish for, you would carefully consider the car you want and would most probably present him with a list detailing everything you desire in a car of your choice: the brand, the model, the year of manufacture, the upholstery color, the external paint job and virtually anything you can think of.

The only reason you would describe your dream car would be because you know and believe that your father can provide for your desires and needs.

Faith is exactly the same.

You can liken this entire story to you and God.

God is the Father in this story while we humans are the children. God, our Father can provide anything we want, because it's all within His power... everything ever created, all that exists are controlled by Him. If only we can exercise our faith and be specific in what we ask from Him.

"But if you remain in me and my words remain in you, you may ask for anything you want, and it will be granted!"

John 15:7 (NLT)

Now, what if the son did not believe his father. Perhaps the son felt his father did not love him and that he would not keep his word; or perhaps the father is just apathetic and does not really pay attention to his son's desires and wishes; perhaps he had promised him things before in the past but did not deliver...

The son's request might be simple and would most probably not include a list; perhaps he would just ask for a car, any car, and maybe (just maybe) he would not even have asked' since he was sure and convinced that his father was not serious with his proposition.

If you then, evil (sinful by nature) as you are, know how to give good and advantageous gifts to your children, how much more will your Father who is in heaven [perfect as He is] give what is good and advantageous to those who keep on asking Him.

Matthew 7:11 (AMP)

The Contract

"I believe God's word. He is my heavenly father," I said to myself.

Eventually, I wrote a contract with God in my favorite bible... some sort of agreement between me and Him, like many men did in the bible (They were called covenants back then) It was a contract to make me focus on Him and serve Him better; a vision that would help me keep my eyes on Him.

The contract went something like this:

"Lord If you give me all your blessings in your word I will give you all my strength, mind and talents."

And so, it began... over the next year, I compiled- and made a list of everything I wanted in life. I told God I wanted to prosper and grow in influence. This part of the contract I had copied from the contract Jabez made in *1 Chronicles 4:10*.

I also began to write what I wanted in the wife that I wanted Him to find for me; I followed the challenge on the radio program.

As time passed, my list became more and more specific. I made it less vague, and I clearly defined what I wanted; the kind of house I wanted and the things in it; the attributes that I desired in the woman that would be my wife.

I took time and asked myself:

"What is it that I REALLY want?"

I made a game plan for what I wanted in my future wife. I divided my desires for her attributes into 3 sections: physical, mental and spiritual.

For physical attributes, I noted down the height I wanted, the skin color and even the location that I wanted her to have been born in.

For mental attributes, I asked for a peaceful phlegmatic (stolidly calm disposition) wife, since I figured that I was quick-tempered and impatient and a wife with a temper like mine would not really work out. I needed someone who could cope with me and handle my temper without worsening whatever situation we were in. There had to be a balance within my marriage relationship.

For spiritual attributes, I noted down in my list that I wanted a mature Christian woman who was not afraid of a potential call to ministry; a call to serve the Lord and be useful and instrumental in advancing His kingdom.

By the time the list was complete, I had written down over 30 specific attributes that I wished for- and desired in her.

I had made a mould of my future wife; an exact image of what she would be like.

The mould helped me sort through my youthful passions and helped me to stay focused. The list helped me to navigate the waves of different ladies that came my way through my journey. Anytime I would meet a girl whom I felt attracted to, I would observe whether she fit the criteria that I had set and had the attributes that I desired.

The easiest and fastest way to do this was to determine whether she fit into the physical mould I had created: if she was not **5' 4"** tall and had thick curvy black hair and a strong Spanish accent, I would move on and not try to pursue her.

This strategy assisted me in avoiding quite a number of toxic and unstable people that the rest of my peers would constantly and ignorantly pursue, and which usually led to heartbreaks and frustrations for them. I had decided to wait on the Lord and not settle for anything less than my dream woman. This would require some discipline on my part, and so the waiting game began. I believed that God could give me all I wanted.

I want to explain something very important I figure out here. I learned this from Godly wise words from the book of Proverbs. Think of the consequences of what you ask for. For example, if I asked for a Lamborghini in my teens, the odds of me crashing and killing myself would have increased significantly. Would I want to take that risk? Wisdom tells me "**NO**!"

Or let's say you asked for a husband that is very intelligent and book-smart. Are you okay with being proved in the wrong most of the time because he knows how to reason well? I know a man that asked for a wife to borderline worship him. I just rolled my eyes. I can see a mess coming with that one...

Do you want a wife that is unable to make decisions on her own? Or maybe she would be insecure and wouldn't let you hang out with the guys because she wants to be with you all the time.

I chose vinyl siding when I planned the kind of house I wanted, the reason being that I wanted a house that I could easily take care of.

These are the type of questions and things you want to think of when you make your list of what you really want from God. Don't be in a hurry, time and maturity will often reveal what we truly want in our life.

Sometimes our needs and desires will develop and change; don't frustrate yourself, ask God for Wisdom to choose those things that will be a blessing in your life

And from this Chapter, I would like you to note that if you want something to work in your life, you need to be serious with it. Have a plan; decide on what exactly you want; be specific about it. Think deep and true, search yourself and find out what you truly want and need. You also want to think about the possible effects that the things you want will cause, then put down every single detail that is involved in your desire.

You have to trust Him; put your faith in Him with no reservations; you have to be convinced that he can do exactly what you want Him to do; you need to have complete faith and trust in His love for you, and you need to be ready to do His wishes; to walk in His way; to delight in Him and His words.

You also need to have a focused attitude and be able to ignore all the distractions that come your way, because they WILL come... and for you to accomplish your goal and not get derailed, you need to stay on track and have your eyes on your objectives.

Reflection

Questions for Chapter 3

Answer the following questions taken from this section, and focus your mind

Write down your answers and thoughts

1. What does wisdom mean to you?

_____

_____

_____

_____

_____

_____

_____

_____

2. Where did your advice and wisdom come from growing up?

_____

_____

_____

_____

_____

_____

_____

_____

_____

3. How has your willingness to be open to direction and advice affected your life?

_____

_____

_____

_____

_____

_____

_____

_____

_____

4. How do you define faith?

_____

_____

_____

_____

_____

_____

_____

_____

5. What are some of the challenges to living a life of faith?

_____

_____

_____

_____

_____

_____

_____

_____

_____

6. Write down a short list of what your 100% sure you want in life.

_____

_____

_____

_____

_____

_____

_____

_____

_____

_____

Chapter 4

The Heartbreaks Begin (Ages 17-21)

One of the many great mistakes young people make is that they tend to be impatient and often lack self-control. Youth make many emotional decisions without really thinking about the implications. This usually leads to them experiencing unnecessary heart-aches and pain.

As we mature, we learn that it is better to wait for something with great value than to settle for something mediocre which usually ends in regret down the line. I figured this out quite early in life because I observed this impatience and lack of self-control in many of my peers, who hastily made decisions such as this without really considering the implications weeks, months and years later.

There were also times when the impulses were just too overwhelming for me, resulting in me erring and suffering a couple of heartbreaks in the process.

While in high school, I met a young lady with whom I built a friendship. She did not fit my physical mould, but with my expecting to get my desires quickly I let my emotions begin to cloud the agreement that I had made with God. I invested in and pursued the relationship with selfish motives.

"She is beautiful and Godly so maybe she is going to be my future wife", I would say to myself.

I didn't consider whether we were compatible. I couldn't care less whether I had the temperament that she needed in the guy that God had in mind for her.

"However," a voice kept telling me, *"she does not fit the rest of the mould; therefore, she is not the perfect match; she's not what you're looking for."*

I began to make excuses about why she would be mine. I chose to ignore the voice and carry on with my selfish agenda. I would buy her expensive gifts for her birthday, go out of my way and do favors for her all the time. Meanwhile, she wouldn't do anything for me. In fact, she would often shoot me these looks that made me feel like a piece of garbage. She had the ability to make me feel like a million bucks only to make me feel unloved and unimportant the next day.

Because of my low self-esteem, I didn't make my move to date her. I figured that I would become her best friend, then make my move when we got older. I thought she would be captivated by my amazing persona by then...

Boy, was I wrong! Our friendship would hit many bad moments where we wouldn't talk to each other for months because of a fight we would have. I would think to myself that she would reach out to me and apologize, or try and mend the relationship, but she never did. In fact, I was the one always reaching out to her.

It was those moments that would open my eyes and make me realize that she was not for me.

Sadly, my youthful impulses would lead me back to her and the cycle would repeat itself.

After 8 years of pursuing her on and off, spending hundreds of dollars on her, and investing many years of hope, it all came to an end one day with extreme and devastating heartbreak. She had not dated a guy for years while we were friends in high school. I felt that I would be the lucky person to date her. Once we graduated, I was ready to make my move. My self-esteem was at an all-time high and I felt ready.

I reached out to her mom for advice. I let her know that I liked her daughter. She told me that she would ask me not to confess my love for her until she was done with college; she didn't want her daughter to be distracted in her studies, and I agreed.

Then came our first year in college. She attended Northcentral University in Minneapolis and I attended Bethel University across town. As we talked on the phone one day she confessed to me that she had started dating a mutual friend of ours; a friend we both agreed was a jerk and was a bad deal. The guy had an extremely bad record with girls. He had emotionally bankrupted the lives of all the girls he'd ever dated. What made it even worse was the fact that she knew this. I knew she was about to be his next victim.

The news hit me harder than I had ever expected. I felt like my life was over; alone and unwanted; I didn't want to live anymore. I had attached myself to her so emotionally that it tore me apart so bad that I had to seek out a College Campus Pastor immediately at that very moment. I left my dorm room bawling my eyes out like never before and running out to the Pastors office.

I told him how I felt cheated and unwanted. I was upset with God, he wasn't being attentive, I thought. I wanted things to go my way for my plans to come to fruition. I took my affairs out of His hand and assumed control all because I was frustrated.

The sad thing is that the whole thing was my fault. I had gotten impatient and hasty which had resulted in me making hasty and emotional decisions over and over. I engulfed myself in a world of fantasy with her, I only dreamed of what could happen one day, when all along God said "**NO.**"

Despite all of this, I knew deep down inside of me that God cares and always will. I eventually came to terms with this and chose to completely trust in Him, in His plans, His abilities.

I said to Him: *"Lord, you know best and I will trust you"*.

Whenever I would become desperate and frustrated; whenever my faith flickered and I derailed from my plan; and whenever I began to pursue a girl that did not fit into my criteria and did not possess the attributes I desired.

God always seemed to know how to get my attention and reminded me that she was not my dream girl; he always knew how to get me back on track. He knew how to make me see that I was going about it the wrong way.

I learned to wait on the Lord. Even more, I became more patient and more trusting in Him. This one time I got to know a girl at my church. I approached her and told her that I wanted to get to know her and within two weeks of getting to know each other, of talking about each other and understanding each other's perspectives, she tells me, "*Ay un muchacho en la Iglesia queue me quire*", which translates as, "*there is a boy at the church that likes me.*"

Of course, this did not phase me. I wasn't in the least bit surprised.

The following week after she told me about the boy, I found out that she had started dating him. A few weeks later, I started to hear from people that she was not happy with the boy and they were having problems. I then heard that her parents would not let her cut it off with the guy because he was a new Christian. They did not want him to get discouraged and lose his faith because of her, which would have most probably ended in him leaving the Church.

She had made a hasty decision to jump into a relationship, a common enough problem amongst youths because of their lack of patience. She had not been able to wait and now she was stuck in a relationship she no longer was interested in.

And then one day some time later, after Church, she came up to me with a sad expression on her face. I could see that she was feeling terrible.

"*Why didn't you wait?*" I asked her.

She burst into tears and could not control herself. I walked away feeling quite proud of myself and what I had accomplished. I felt like a boss. Yes, I said it; I had gotten a glimpse into the heart of a heartbreaker, which is not the right heart to have by the way. I had realized the importance of waiting and making wise decisions.

Ask yourself how many relationships you have gotten into, only to regret ever getting into them in the first place. Your willingness to wait is extremely important to get all you want in your life.

As months rolled into years and my desires were still not fulfilled, I again became faint of heart and began to question Gods promises for me that he gave us in His word. However, only His word would give me the comfort I needed. I read in **Proverbs**:

"Hope deferred maketh the heart sick: but when the desire cometh, it is a tree of life"

Proverbs 13:12 (KJV)

My faith in Him and the list that I had prepared began to wane. I began to doubt if I was ever going to get the desires of my heart; if he was ever going to fulfil His part of the bargain and give me what I wanted, I began to lose hope and become impatient once again.

Moral - This chapter tells about my lack of impatience and what I had suffered for it, if you give a job to God to do for you, let Him handle it, do not try to assume control for yourself. You need to be patient, give Him control of the car and take the back seat, and let Him direct your affairs. When walking with God, you need to be patient. You should not try to control your circumstances, no, you need to trust Him completely and believe that he will accomplish what you want in His time. He sees what you do not; he has a bigger plan than you could ever begin to fathom. Know and trust that He is always working on your behalf; give Him the space. Be patient and steadfast in your trust and faith in Him.

Think about it this way, he knows where the landmines are, if you move without His direction, the odds of you getting hurt go up every time you move without his direction. God is the Scout you need, to move through this thing called "**Life**"; He knows the way to get you the desires of your heart.

Reflection

Questions for Chapter 4

Answer the following questions taken from this section, and focus your mind

Write down your answers and thoughts

1. How has your stubbornness hurt your life?

_____

_____

_____

_____

_____

_____

_____

_____

_____

_____

_____

2. How does your lack of emotional control hurt your life?

_____

_____

_____

_____

_____

_____

_____

_____

_____

_____

_____

_____

_____

3. How do you handle discouragement?

_____

_____

_____

_____

_____

_____

_____

_____

_____

_____

_____

_____

Chapter 5

Lima, Peru

Time was running out with the agreement I made with God, I was getting older and my plans were getting behind schedule. It was my heart's desire to be married by the time I was 25 years old (that was the plan I had laid down on my contract with God).

I wanted to be a young father, to run and play with my kids, to know this joy early in life; the joy of having kids and nurturing them; of watching them grow up; of setting them on their life paths...

I knew I had to date a girl for at least a year, court her and get an insight into who she really is, how compatible we are, before I got married to her... so when I turned 23 and still had not found the woman of my dreams, I did some calculations and I realized that time was almost up and that if I were to have any chance of achieving this huge dream, the time to find that woman was immediately.

Then something occurred that I saw as a breakthrough of sorts. A new girl began to attend my church and she had all the physical attributes on my list; she totally fit into the mould I had created. There were just two really huge problems hindering me from taking any action with her. Firstly, she was a new Christian just beginning to develop and grow in her faith; my list said that she had to be a mature believer, already deeply steeped in her faith. I did some more calculations and it appeared that I would have to wait for at least another year as she developed and blossomed fully into her faith.

"Don't team up with those who are unbelievers."

2 Corinthians 6:14 (NLT)

The second and even more serious problem was that she was already engaged to be married! I held my feelings closely and guarded it like a big secret in my heart. I felt forced to look elsewhere and consider other options.

Meanwhile, I had a friend at work named *Armando* who always tried to hook me up with different kinds of girls. They were beautiful but not Christians and that was a deal breaker for me because it totally went against my list. My friend was an older man in his fifties from **Lima, Peru**. Where is that you say? It is over by *Brazil* and *Argentina* somewhere on the South American continent. *Lima* is the capital of *Peru* and it lies on the shore of the **Pacific**. I had never heard of that place in my entire life.

My friend introduced me to a dating website that had many beautiful and exotic girls from **Lima, Peru**. That sounds crazy, right? I was shopping online for my dream girl, like a person shops for groceries at the store; this must be Gods plan for me, I said to myself. One of the attributes I desired and noted on my list was that my woman had to have a heavy foreign accent; *this was it,* I thought to myself, because who better to have the accent I wanted than a woman from Peru? (Although, my list specifically stated she had to be a *Mexican* woman from around the *Jalisco* area)

With this new and wondrous tool at my fingertips (literally), my search took on a completely new direction and got infused with new enthusiasm and excitement. I was eager to try this new thing out and see what results I would get and how it would work out. I was hopeful that I would get my wishes fulfilled through this platform. I set up my profile with every bit of honesty I could muster. I included every detail I could conceive and seemed important. I painted as accurate a picture as possible of myself. I even included that one of my favorite movies was *Happy Feet*. Yes, a cartoon that most adults would be embarrassed to even associate themselves with, since cartoons are considered to be for kids.

For those thinking that it was a bad move, guess what: you are wrong. Because this particular fact on my profile was what caught the attention of *Miss Cecilia Amanda Vasquez* (not her real last names).

Now to be honest, the only reason I originally took interest in her profile was because of her eyes, since the cover picture was only her left eye and her nose. Strange that any person would be interested in someone and start a friendship based on just one eye and a nose, right?

Yes, it was a shot in the dark, I knew that. But I was still willing to take that shot. The game was on, I was in it now and fully ready to play.

We began emailing each other; we sent emails back and forth during the whole work day. We averaged hundreds of emails every day for the next couple of months, we were quite taken with each other, learning all that there was to learn about one another.

Finally, I asked her if we could talk on the phone and she agreed.

I called her as soon I got the chance.

Her voice and accent were so pleasing to my ears that I felt myself melting like a Popsicle on the fourth of Duly (Darla, little rascals). I fell head over heels in love with her... or so I thought.

She was a mature Christian woman and was not afraid of a call to ministry. We talked and conversed for hours every Sunday evening as calling cards were quite expensive at the time.

The more we talked and got to know each other, the more I fell for her, the more I felt myself thinking and wishing that she was the one I had been searching for. The only thing that was left for me was to see a picture of her and what she really looked like.

Now for those who do not know: **Lima, Peru** is a third world country. And as at that time, there was an ongoing battle with local guerrilla fighters. Also, they had a poor internet service which was not very strong for local residents. *Cecilia* did not have a cell phone with picture capabilities, much less internet capabilities. She had to rely on super slow dial-up service from her home computer and it usually took her about 20 minutes just to access the internet.

A couple months later she finally sent me a full body shot of herself. The picture quality was quite low and it was apparent from the get-go that she did not fit the physical requirements I had set for my woman on my list.

Her hair was thin and straight, her nose was bigger than I desired. These attributes conflicted with my list, they were the exact opposites of what I had listed. My youthful impulse took over though and I pushed ahead instead of drawing back. I told myself that she was still beautiful and her accent was still there, a plus for her. I began to lose faith in the list, like I had done a number of times already; and I once again began to lose faith in God's promises; to lose sight of what mattered. I would make it work my way, I said. I would accomplish my goals myself.

Meanwhile, at church, I heard a word from the Lord. The Lord said:

"Te la entrego, Pero ser paciente porque voy a tratar con su corrazon", which translates to, "I give her to you, be patient for I will work in her heart."

I assumed that the Lord was telling me about *Cecilia*, that this message was meant to tell me that she was mine that the Lord would work on her and she would eventually fall madly in love with me.

Now *Cecilia* was not perfect and had her own flaws, there were certain aspects of her personality, certain characteristics of hers that showed great selfishness and immaturity. These attributes went against my list. But I ignored them and did not care. I wanted her all the same, despite all of this; I trusted that the Lord would work on these things and change her heart.

Six months later I made the decision to pay her a visit in Peru. My family members and church members thought I was crazy. They could not understand how I could decide to travel so many miles to see someone I did not really know; someone I had never seen before. Everybody told me not to go because it could turn out to be a trap... I could end up being kidnapped... but I simply did not care. My mind was made up, I was going to do it no matter what everybody said; I refused to be discouraged and to instead push forward and be persistent.

During this time, I had become the Youth Pastor at my church. The girl that joined my church and fitted my criteria (and was engaged to be married) began to work with me in the youth group. We got close and began a friendship. I told her about Cecilia and how I felt about her; my hopes and aspirations concerning her. She would give me advice about her and I in turn would give her advice about her fiancé. I always kept my heart from giving her selfish advice; I did my utmost to give her really helpful advice.

I put on the tunnel vision goggles and headed out on the journey to meet Cecilia in Lima Peru. The craziness of it all did not hit me until I got on the airliner heading to Lima; I had not had a doubt at all or considered the things that could go wrong and their implications. I looked around me on the plane and told myself, "**Are you crazy, what are you doing?**"

Everyone around me on the plane looked quite different from me. Almost all of them were short and had broad shoulders. I soon realized that *Lima* has a heavy population of Japanese descendants. I wish I could say that I was super cool about that which I really was not. I was almost hyperventilating thinking about it. The thought came to my mind that *Cecilia* could be a fake person. What if I *did* get kidnapped? What if this entire thing was just an elaborate scam with me as the victim? Perhaps she did not look at all like her pictures...

My thoughts were running wild on the plane to *Lima*; it was like all the bad thoughts had waited for me to get on that plane before deciding to rear their ugly heads.

I consoled myself by telling myself that if something looked suspicious and malicious, if she did not look like her pictures, I would run to the police. I quickly calmed down and felt better.

I had been impatient and I took matters into my own hands again, I rebelled against God, while deceiving myself that it was His wish, I deluded myself into thinking that what I was doing was what he wished for and that I had His support, I tweaked signs that he did not give me all for my own benefit. I became selfish, although I trusted Him. I wanted to hurry things up; to try and assist Him doing His job. I used my own wisdom instead of His Wisdom. My plan was to get married by age 25 and in my own mind and my own calculations, God was working slowly for my liking and my benefit. I tried to speed things up again.

Trust in the Lord with all your heart and lean not on your own understanding; in all your ways submit to Him, and He will make your paths straight.

Proverbs 3:5 (KJV)

Let these words be a warning to you: a warning that no matter how tempted you are, no matter how helpful you want to be and however wise you seem to be, it's always better to let Him handle your affairs.

Often, the more educated or successful we become in life the more we begin to rely on our own knowledge, feelings and ability to do things. Little do people realize that we are replacing God's place in our life with the idol called "**yourself**."

God wants to give you the desires of your heart. He doesn't want to hurt you, he wants you to trust Him and he will make it easier for you. Trust Him, even if it looks like it's all falling apart.

But blessed is the one who trusts in the LORD, whose confidence is in Him

Jeremiah 17:7 (NIV)

Reflection

Questions for Chapter 5

Answer the following questions taken from this section, and focus your mind

Write down your answers and thoughts

1. Relate an incident or example of something you convinced yourself was of God/good when it was not

._____

_____

_____

_____

_____

_____

_____

_____

_____

_____

_____

_____

_____

_____

_____

_____

_____

_____

_____

_____

_____

2. How has your own wisdom and knowledge led you to make bad decisions?

_____

_____

_____

_____

_____

_____

_____

_____

_____

_____

_____

_____

_____

_____

_____

_____

_____

_____

_____

_____

Chapter 6

Cecilia

Before I left, Cecilia and I had agreed that she would meet me at the airport with her parents. I wanted to impress them right away, something I had learned to do as a youth Pastor when dealing with parents, and so I came dressed in a black suit and white shirt with a large dress coat

I felt really good about myself while descending from the plane, confident like I had a million dollars. It also helped to boost my morale and self-esteem that I was taller than most people there. Part of me felt like a famous basketball player walking among the much shorter locals.

I wish I could say that it was love at first sight. I wish I could say that the moment I laid my eyes on Cecilia, I felt wowed and taken with her. As I stepped down from the plane, I looked out to the crowd of people waiting for their loved ones at the airport corridor. I scanned through them searching for a nervous and beautiful girl. I never expected to feel what I felt next. I was expecting to feel ecstatic and stunned but as I scanned the sea of people I noticed a young girl who was around the same age as I (age 24 at the time) that fit the description of Cecilia. She had an extremely nervous look about her and the first thing I noticed about her was the nose, it seemed to be off a bit, like it was broken. It had a bump and appeared tilted.

She also had braces and this did not help my opinion of her at that point at all. Her face had a distinct *Peruvian* look, which I was not used to seeing, and the first thought that came to my mind was that she wasn't as attractive as I expected. I wasn't too disappointed since I had prepared myself for the worst.

I also noticed a nervous looking grown man beside her, whom I could easily tell was her father. I briskly walked over to them where they were standing and introduced myself first to her, after which I turned to her father and did the same.

He quickly walked us out of the airport to a taxi. My initial plan was to stay at a motel near their house but *Cecilia* gave me a heads up that her father planned to host me in their spare room so that he could keep a close eye on me and properly monitor me. As I sat next to *Cecilia* in the taxi I told myself that we were just friends and that this was going to be a nice trip that I would enjoy. I was in a foreign country after all and I had never been there before, I would go out and soak in the sights. This made me feel relaxed.

Cecilia and I were both mature Christians and we had been praying about our relationship for a while by then. She was a believer in signs from God, she believed that God communicated His wishes to us through certain signs and all we had to do was recognize them.

I was not so much a believer of such. She once told me about a time that she was praying and fasting about me trying to confirm whether I was God's gift to her. She told me that as she was praying in a taxi one day, asking for signs from God, she looked up and noticed out the window of the taxi a restaurant with the name Victor on it. I just rolled my eyes and told myself: "***whatever works to make you mine***". I did not really care about the details or specifics, all I cared about was getting her as my girl; I was less concerned about how it happened.

By this time, I had decided to get things done by myself as I felt as if God was taking too long to answer me again and so I would make it happen myself. I remember telling God once to just give her to me and that even if she was not ready I would deal with the consequences and cope with her while he works on her. That advice was not me on a normal day, it is not something I would normally support... but it was how I felt on that particular day. It was my rebellious side coming out and rearing its head for the umpteenth time.

I felt relaxed as we got in the taxi and headed to her house. As I sat in the taxi I looked over at **Cecilia** as she sat there silently. I noticed how nervous and scared she was and I began to have compassion for her. She was wonderfully made by God and she was beautiful in her own way. I began to notice features on her face that were different, but beautiful.

They were not features that I was familiar with since I had never met a girl from *Peru* before but they were beautiful nonetheless. I could not in all honesty expect her to look like the girls I was familiar with. I realized that different people from different places had their own distinct and unique features that distinguished them from other people from other places.

Daylight had given way to darkness as we approached her home. I can remember driving through dirt roads and catching a glimpse of a small stucco entrance. I could not see much as it was really dark and there was no light post on the streets. I remember walking into her house, looking up and noticing that there was no roof and assuming that they were poor. Then we walked a bit further in and I discovered that they had roofs and the building outside was just the courtyard.

They quickly showed me to the room they had prepared for me. Cecilia had already told me that her dad wanted me close by so that he could keep an eye on me. I did not have a problem with that, although I knew that he had nothing to fear. But still, he was her father and would definitely do everything within his power to protect her. I could not blame him for wanting to protect his family. To them I was a total stranger. Just as much as they were to me.

I walked into the room I was given, closed the door and let it all sink in, the fact that I was there, in Lima Peru having travelled over so many miles to visit a girl I had never before seen in my life.

When I came out of the room, I saw Cecilia sitting by herself at the table. I walked over to where she sat and took my seat. All I desired at this point was just to build a friendship with her; I had already taken my mind off her being my woman. I then realized that she was still quite nervous.

She opened her mouth and with her exotic accent told me, "*I can't believe this*".

I looked into her eyes and then took out my cell phone. I pretended to call her and converse with her the way we had been doing for the past six months.

As I pretended to talk to her on the phone I was able to lessen her tension and make her less nervous. *Cecilia* looked at me with amazement (the first time that a girl had looked at me with such wonder and awe in her eyes and to be honest, it felt amazing).

She then told me, "**You are amazing, you know**". And that statement, coupled with the adorable accent and look was what it took to push me over the edge. I started to fall in love with her again. That is what interest in a person can do. It can make them feel loved and good about themselves, almost invincible.

There is a saying: "**every man needs a woman to fight for**."

A man can accomplish anything, go any number of miles to achieve something, even conquer the world when he has the respect and belief of his woman, a woman that deeply loves her man and supports him greatly. That support is setting him up to achieve great things because this does a great deal for the man's self-confidence and belief in himself and his abilities. Support for a man by his woman fills him with almost superhuman strength. This belief in him then translates to determination to achieve whatever it is he sets out to do.

As a young man growing up, I found myself easily influenced and affected by this strong emotion. I had seen a lot of manifestations of it, especially on television. I remember that in ROCKY II, Rocky could not find or muster the will and courage to fight Apollo Creed, until Adrian woke up from her coma. She then softly uttered the words to Rocky, "**Win-Win.**"

These words became the call to action that he had lacked. Her words served to motivate and saturate him with the determination and motivation he needed to become the champion of the world. Definitely, people had tried to encourage him, definitely he had tried to muster courage within himself about this battle but ultimately, what it took was the support, faith and trust of a woman, his woman.

This particular saying also works the other way around. When a woman diminishes the value of her man and speaks negative, unflattering words to him she shows him she does not believe in him. She calls him things like, "**You are a loser**" or "**My mother was right, I should not have married you.**"

You cut the legs off from under him and leave him flapping in the wind. You damage his self-believe, self-esteem and ability to perform. If he was not performing well before, he will definitely perform even less after the discouraging and morale damaging words that he has been fed. Deep inside every man, there is a scared and insecure little boy always doubting himself.

"**Am I good enough?**" he asks himself every day, trying to prove himself to those around him.

The next two days that I spent there in **Lima, Peru** were some of the best days of my life up to that particular point. I fell in love with **Cecilia** with every part of my being; it was like a fairy tale come to life.

By the 3rd day of being there, I had succeeded in convincing myself that she was God's gift to me. I convinced myself that she had been handed over to me by Him, to marry.

But I knew deep down that she did not fit my list. There were many red flags that I was ignoring, but those red flags would soon reveal their true face. There were plenty of warning signs but I chose to ignore them. I was completely in love and utterly infatuated with her.

"A prudent person foresees danger and takes precautions. The simpleton goes blindly on and suffers the consequences."

Proverbs 27:12 (NLT)

I could have heeded the warning signs and gone on my way; stopped the direction things were going and kept to my plan but no: I was too stubborn and fixed with myself to take note of anything, I just pressed on like a blind fool going into traffic with no guide.

I was quite foolish and rebellious; I ignored things that were right in front of my eyes that were supposed to make me stop on the path I was walking. I continued in my delusion and rebellion towards God, convincing myself that it was His wish; the way He wanted things to go; that things were progressing according to His plan.

There is a lesson to be taken from here, listen to God's voice in whatever you do. Make sure he approves and that it is His wish. That still small voice inside of you is

God's way of guiding you and speaking to you; don't ignore it. Do not just jump into things thinking and trying to convince yourself that it's entirely His plan, just because you want it to be so. You would only waste your time and hurt yourself that way because if that does work out, you would have deprived yourself of something better.

Reflection

Questions for Chapter 6

Answer the following questions taken from this section, and focus your mind

Write down your answers and thoughts

1. Why do we often try to do things on our own?

_____

_____

_____

_____

_____

_____

_____

_____

_____

_____

_____

2. Why is following your feelings on decisions, such bad advice?

_____

_____

_____

_____

_____

_____

_____

_____

_____

_____

_____

3. Why do you think people still choose not listen to advice even though their life is falling into a spiral?

_____

_____

_____

_____

_____

_____

_____

_____

_____

_____

_____

Chapter 7

Falling In, Falling Out Of "Love"

By the end of the 3rd day of my stay, I had decided to go ahead and make her the one, the woman I would marry and build a family with. I went ahead and asked her to marry me, I also asked her father to bless and approve of our relationship.

The problem, though, was that she did not want to date yet. She was not sure what she wanted between us- she did not even know how to describe what was between us to her father or even herself, she was confused. And then the day after that which happened to be the 4th day of my stay in **Lima, Peru**, everything fell apart.

Cecilia had decided to meet with her Pastor that morning regarding our relationship. I was excited, because I felt that our relationship was moving by leaps and bounds. I had expected the Pastor to bless her decision and encourage us to move forward, which in my head meant to form a legitimate dating relationship and begin to make plans for marriage.

That afternoon I met up with *Cecilia* to talk about how the meeting went. I was excited and filled with hope; hope that God was giving me the woman of my dreams and desires.

Cecilia began to tell me what the Pastor said. The Pastor had told her that according to how she described our relationship thus far, we were already dating. I smiled and nodded my head in agreement and satisfaction. She told me how the Pastor had given her two options: either make our relationship formal and continue dating or cut it off with me and for her to join the church leadership again and wait for God to bring the right guy to her.

Cecilia asked: *"Sabes cual escogí (do you know which one I choose)?"* I shrugged my shoulders playfully, thinking she was being sarcastic and trying to make me nervous, because, of course, she was choosing me! She said, *"escogí la segunda opción (I chose the second option)."*

I froze. A strong feeling of disbelief and anger began to bubble inside of me. I repeated what she just said to me.

"Are you serious?" I then asked her, hoping to hear "*gotcha!*"

However, she only became serious and repeated her decision. She continued to tell me that she wanted us to just be friends and nothing more; that maybe things could change in the future.

I let it sink in for a couple of minutes. I felt my heart break in pieces for the second time in my life. Her rejection did not feel good at all. I felt devastated for I knew that if I could not conquer her heart there and convince her to marry me, if I could not make her say "**yes**" while I was with her in person, I had absolutely no hope of accomplishing it from a long distance.

I lost control and cried like a baby, asking her why she was playing games with my heart, why she was hurting me and making me sad. To be honest, that was not my proudest moment. In fact, it probably was one of the most selfish and most embarrassing moments in my life. I even cried harder so she would cry, which she eventually did. I wanted to hurt her too, to make her feel guilty for breaking my heart and hurting my feelings. I wanted to make her feel horrible for dashing my hopes. She hurt me, so I would hurt her back.

When we got home that night, we both went directly to our respective rooms. *Cecilia*'s parents were home when we arrived and our cold behavior and attitude towards each other certainly did not go unnoticed. I stayed in my room for the rest of that day and into the next.

The next day, which was the 5th day, happened to be my last day with *Cecilia*. I was traveling home that night.

Cecilia went out to work very early even before I woke up. That morning her parents and I talked about what had transpired between me and their daughter. I poured out the contents of my broken heart while they listened attentively. They didn't know what to say. Later in the day, Cecilia came back home from work. We had planned to go to church together that evening and I asked her if I could still come with her and she agreed.

I was trying my best to understand what was happening to us, what was changing, because everything was going perfectly until now. No signal that we would find ourselves at this stage that we were.

I began telling God how I felt, confided in Him about my problems. I was sad and devastated, yet I chose to trust God a little longer; to believe that he could still make things work and intervene. I had tried things my way and it had not panned out the way I wanted. I had no choice but to trust in Him; to put my faith in Him.

After all, he was my father and he cared deeply for me. Trusting God was the best thing I knew to do when life became uncertain, it was what gave me strength, hope and courage when things got tough. I placed my trust in Him again at this point because I did not know what else to do, no one else to turn to and confide in so, I cast all my worries on Him.

"My righteous ones will live by faith. But I will take no pleasure in anyone who turns away.

"Hebrews 10:38 (NLT)

For me, trusting God was not a fairy-tale idea, it was not a thing that just existed in my fantasies, something to be done reluctantly. Trusting God was an action, a verb, it was something that needed to be acted out, and it was something real, tangible and substantial. When we got to Church that afternoon, I could have chosen to just sit down where I was with a sad face. I could have wallowed in self-pity and sadness while everyone else stood to worship the Lord. I knew that there was no other way to show my trust (faith) in the Lord than to get to my feet and praise Him. I stood up and I worshiped Him as if I did not have a care in the world, like all my worries and sadness were simply non-existent. I stood there and believed that God is not a God of confusion and that he had His plans and His ways of accomplishing them. I showed my faith and trust in Him through my actions, I engaged actively in His worship.

The Bible tells us that he is the God of direction and guidance, that he will show us the way when we truly trust and have faith in Him.

"Trust in the LORD with all your heart and lean not on your own understanding; in all your ways submit to Him, and he will make your paths straight."

Proverbs 3:5-6 (NIV)

"Thy word is a lamp unto my feet, and a light unto my path."

Psalm 119:105 (KJV)

God has nothing but good things in store for us. We just have to know when to let go and let Him. His plans for us are greater than our plans for ourselves; he knows what is best for us and what is harmful to us, what we need the most and when we need it. He knows everything and he cares, whatever he does is for our own good, we might not see it, we might not know how or even understand it but His plan for us is good. Every event in our lives lead us towards His grand plan, he is not confused nor does he seek to confuse us. All we need to do is submit to Him, trust in Him completely and give way to His will and plans.

"For I know the plans I have for you, declares the LORD, plans to prosper you and not to harm you, plans to give you hope and a future."

Jeremiah 29:11 (NIV)

If God does not confuse us then people must be the problem, we must be the reason why we are confused, we must be the ones that confuse ourselves. People are the ones prone to errors, the ones that ignore the warnings and signs that are there to guide us. We are the ones that let our emotions control us and let rational and critical thinking fly out the window. We are the ones that lie and delude ourselves into believing what we deeply know is not true. We humans are the ones that want to believe what others say about us, no matter how untrue and false it is. We are the ones that choose to believe that God does not love us, that he is not capable of taking care of us, and even when the truth is right in front of us and is glaring, we still grasp at what is comfortable, even though it is not true.

As I stood there in the Church, I heard a powerful voice in my spirit speak to me. I heard God tell me:

"Give her back to me."

At that moment, my mind went to the story of Abraham and Isaac when God asked Him to sacrifice His son. At the end of that story, God let Him keep His son after testing His faith. I comforted myself by telling myself that this was the case here. It was all a test of my trust (faith) in God as it had been a test of Abraham's faith. I smiled and agreed, "**Ok God, you** *can have her back"*, thinking to myself that I will surely get her back when he was satisfied that I had faith in Him.

Then I heard another powerful voice in my spirit say:

"You don't know if I will give her back to you"

I broke down on the floor crying at what was said because it dawned on me at that moment exactly what God was telling me. She was not mine, she had never been, and He was taking her away from me forever, never to be returned. It was not a test of my faith, it was real.

After the service finished, we left the church and headed home to meet with the family. That night they all took me to the airport to board my flight back home. There was not much talking between Cecilia and myself. We both did not have much to say to each other. It was as though we were at a loss for words. We were like babies that had not yet learned how to speak.

I remember telling myself in comfort, *"God is in control, everything will be fine."*

As I started to say goodbye to her parents at the airport, I noticed that *Cecilia* was very serious and stiff. I hugged her, and as I pulled away, I noticed tears coming down her cheeks, she was crying for me, she was crying because I was leaving. That confirmed to me that she cared. Or else, why would she cry?

It was the first time I had ever seen a woman shed tears over me. Oddly enough, this was comforting. I felt at peace in my heart and told her, "*I'll be back soon*", again letting my desires to be loved over-shadow the fact that God had said "**NO**".

I got back home to *Minnesota* on Saturday. Sunday evenings was when we usually spoke on the phone and talked to each other for hours at a stretch. I was excited and really looking forward to talking to her. Sunday evening came and I called her number but she did not answer. I called her a few times more and yet, there was still no answer. I was worried: I did not know what could have happened.

The next day I looked up her profile on **High 5** (an online social media platform that is like **Facebook** and very popular in **Peru**).

High 5 had a feature on it that allowed you to know the last time someone was online. Her page said that she had been online at the same time I was dialling her number. I figured that since her computer took 20 minutes to turn on and connect to the internet, she would have had time to answer my calls and that she deliberately did not pick up. I realized that she did not want to speak with me and that she was avoiding me.

The next day I called her again, and she picked up. I asked her why she did not answer my calls on Sunday and she told me that she was busy. Then I told her that I noticed she was online on High5 which means she was not as busy as she claimed. She cracked and then told me the truth.

The next words that came out of her mouth were surprising and unexpected, yet they served to open my eyes and close this roller coaster ride for good. She said, "*I didn't want to talk, and I knew if I answered you that you would want to talk*". I then asked her, "*Why didn't you message me when you wanted to talk?*" and she said, "*I don't call people, they call me.*"

And just like that, I closed the door. All the red flags that I had been seeing the whole time finally became reality; I finally saw what God was keeping me away from. *Cecilia*'s heart was extremely selfish and greatly lacked **Wisdom** and compassion, all of which were on my list. I understood why God had said no. He had something better for me.

I finally saw her selfishness and immaturity. It suddenly appeared before me like scales had been lifted from my eyes... surely, they must have been there before but I in my wish and desire for things to work out I must have ignored them. She was a person that did not know what she wanted. She was not focused. This caused a lot of pain and frustration in me; I was saddened and devastated by it. I never called her again after that. I chose to go back to my list and wait on God. I chose to leave it all in His hands; to let Him take the reins of my life and guide me. I finally saw the folly of my ways and how wrong I had been. Things obviously were not working my way, I had tried directing my own life and I had failed again.

It became a lot easier to make this wise decision since I had emotionally given her back to God. I had completely let go of her and so, I could move on and forget about her. She was not mine, she had never been and I finally realized and accepted that fact. I decided to trust God again even though the clock was ticking, even though the time I set to be married was running out and I was not really making any progress on my own. I decided to trust in His decisions and let Him do the work.

I had the same thing happen to me when I was involved in a multilevel marketing business. I started the business when I was 18 years old, I cried when I saw the business plan because I thought I found the secret to wealth!

I told myself, *"God will change this for the best; He will give me everything I need."*

The problem was that it wasn't working. I poured into it for 5 years, only to realize that this was not the vehicle God wanted me to take to fulfil my dreams and desires.

I had deceived myself into believing what was not true. Many of us are tempted to make this mistake when we want things to go our way; we forcefully convince ourselves into thinking that it is His wish, that our chosen path was ordained by Him and that it is His plan for us. This is wrong, but in His infinite mercy and grace He would still take us back even after going astray, like the story of the prodigal son in the Bible.

The son had desired to get out on his own, to take his inheritance and live life the way he wanted. The son eventually comes back to his father because he had squandered all the money given to godless things. The son saw the errors of his ways and came home in repentance.

Let us learn from this story. Don't make the same mistakes many of our friends have made. They squander their life, body, gifts, and abilities on things that are not worth it. We need to exercise patience in everything and carefully listen to His voice, we should be certain that he approves of our steps before we embark on it. I was hasty and the path that my hastiness led me on, however pleasant it might have been, whatever respite it might have given me initially, it eventually led to heartbreak and heartaches which made the initial pleasure pale in comparison

Reflection

Questions for Chapter 7

Answer the following questions taken from this section, and focus your mind

Write down your answers and thoughts

1. What do you do when you get full of doubt and anxiety?

_____

_____

_____

_____

_____

_____

_____

_____

_____

_____

_____

_____

2. What do you do when you lose all hope?

_____

_____

_____

_____

_____

_____

_____

_____

_____

_____

_____

_____

3. What are some words of wisdom you received that you wish you would of applied?

_____

_____

_____

_____

_____

_____

_____

_____

_____

_____

_____

_____

Chapter 8

Broken Deal (Age 24)

I told myself, "You were so close, maybe the girl of your dreams is right around the corner, maybe you will get to meet her soon".

I had one eye set on the new girl at church. Her name was Daysi. By this time, I had started to build a friendship with her and it was growing and becoming strong. She had been in church for at least 2 years now. By this time, she had broken up with her fiancé and was single.

I told myself that maybe she could still be mine, I had faith again. Then everything changed and my new-found hope got dashed against the rocks. Daysi got back with her ex-fiancé and they rekindled their relationship. This time they were more serious with each other. I still had faith though for what else could I have. Then like a quick succession of punches that left me winded and disoriented, they were presented at church and soon became engaged again.

It is pretty much a done deal once a couple officially gets presented in Church. The church gives its whole support to them. Everybody gets behind them and tries to pitch in to help them in any way they can. The Church family starts treating them as if they are married already. Everybody gets excited because people know that there is a wedding on the way, which is a joyful thing. Everybody does their best to keep the couple together.

At this point, something in me broke; it was like I had snapped; like I lost control of myself.

For the first time in my life, I had lost all hope on the list. I felt that God did not really care about my desires. My frustrations and perceived failings got me down and miserable. I remember a particular night, I was driving down an exit ramp going south on 94 E to merge onto 394 W in Minneapolis. I was having one of the most serious conversations with God I had ever had in my life as of at that point. The conversation I had with God would mark my life forever.

My tone and feelings were so tense and held up. I fully expected God to break His silence and speak to me, to reveal to me what was happening, to let me into His plans and let me know where I stood in the scheme of things.

I shouted at the top of my lungs and asked Him: "*What is going on God? What the F*#K is going on?*"

I totally lost control; I was like a man on the brink of insanity ranting and repeating these words until my voice cracked. I felt justified since I had done so much, I had sacrificed a lot and had trusted in Him, I had upheld my end of the bargain, I had lived up to my promises and I felt that He owed me a response. He owed me an explanation, a briefing of what was truly going on. I felt that I was right to demand to know how things were going and where they were heading. However, when I heard nothing in response, when he ignored all my ravings and rantings and did not respond, all I could do was cry.

I want to take this opportunity to say that I never use curse words. I remember only cursing 2-3 times before in my entire life. I was a well-behaved young man by all accounts. Looking back, I can see that this prayer of mine was a relationship defining moment in my life, a cornerstone that will remain evergreen and fresh in my memory. God's silence despite all my complaints that night tested my faith on a completely new level than I was used to. I cried myself to sleep that night.

The next day was Sunday, church time. I can recall the day vividly like it was yesterday. I had started to believe that I would not get the girl of my dreams; that was all she was, a dream; one that would never see the light of day; a dream that I had been a fool for having.

I prepared to go to church, and on my way there I took out my Bible and turned the pages till I got to the page where I had written my contract with God so many years before. As I was walking on the sidewalk to the Church, I paused for a while, I then looked at my list and contract (both of which I wrote on the same page). I tore out the page containing both and ripped it apart into small pieces, I then tossed the torn page onto the ground. I completely gave up hope in accomplishing it.

I told God that even though He did not keep His promise, that even though he did not fulfil His end of the bargain, I would keep mine, I would continue to serve Him with all of my strength, talent, and abilities but that I would not do it happily.

At this point in my life, I was completely devastated and hopeless, while I still believed in God and trusted Him. While I still served Him, I cannot say that I did it completely. I gave up hope in His giving me what I wanted. I felt that maybe he did not really care; maybe he had better things to do, I did not know, because he would not tell me. But I remained steadfast in my faith, I remained trusting in Him. I did not for one moment falter in my faith. I continued to walk His path and go His way. No matter how down we feel, how much disappointment we feel, no matter how let down and ignored we feel. We should hold strong in Him. He does have our best interests at heart, and he never forgets what we need. Instead, he is working to deliver perfection; he is working to provide us with the very best of what he has in store for us. I realized years later that God was working on my faith, pushing it to the next level. Since faith is the currency that God works in, he was helping me deepen my faith so that he could use me in even more powerful ways in the future.

Reflection

Questions for Chapter 8

Answer the following questions taken from this section, and focus your mind

Write down your answers and thoughts

1. What are you willing to go through to live a fulfilling life?

_____

_____

_____

_____

_____

_____

_____

_____

_____

_____

_____

_____

2. What are you willing to let go to get the desires of your life?

_____

_____

_____

_____

_____

_____

_____

_____

_____

_____

3. Who are the people in your life that you can seek
out for encouragement during the hard times?

_____

_____

_____

_____

_____

_____

_____

_____

_____

_____

_____

Chapter 9

Dying Relationship (Ages 24- 25)

I completely let go and let God. This is the best way I could describe this particular chapter.

I sought my joy and fulfilment in God alone, giving up chasing and struggling for a woman. I sought His love and His word in my life, putting all my energy in His work because I knew that even with the discouragement I felt, what I needed was to have God in my life... now more than ever. I knew that I needed Him to be in charge of me and my affairs. He had been the source of all the successes I experienced, the architect of my life, the reason why I was where I was. He was the father I never had, the one that provided me with the love I rarely got. He was the one that took me out of my quiet and dark box and transformed my life. God was the one who gave me confidence and strength to become a Godly strong young man; He was the one who took away my sadness; He taught me how to have love for myself. I was not about to throw all that away, no, rather, I worshipped Him more.

"Blessed is the man who trusts in the LORD, and whose hope is the LORD. For he shall be like a tree planted by the waters, which spreads out its roots by the river, and will not fear when heat comes; But its leaf will be green and will not be anxious in the year of drought, nor will cease from yielding fruit."

Jeremiah 17:7-8 (NKJV)

It was not long after this that I began to hear rumors of conflicts between *Daysi* and her fiancé. Soon after *Daysi* and her fiancé would on individual basis approach me for advice about their relationship. They would explain what they were going through and I would advise them on what to do and how to proceed. I can say with all freedom and honesty, that I gave sincere advice as I spoke to them, I did not in any way try to break up their relationship by giving advice that would in any way destroy what they had. The ironic part was that I had never been in a dating relationship with anyone before, much less engaged. I had virtually been single my whole life, yet here I was giving advice on love and relationships despite my inexperience. God's love had penetrated my soul in such a way that the right words would come out of my mouth, I was well familiar in His wishes and commands that I felt strong convictions on the way to go.

> *"The one who does not love has not become acquainted with God [does not and never did know Him], for God is love. [He is the originator of love, and it is an enduring attribute of His nature.]"*
>
> ### *1 John 4:8 (AMP)*

I started discerning that this relationship did not have much in common. Their desires were not aligned, and I noticed that they were two different people heading two different ways, two different people with two different plans for their individual lives. I felt in my spirit that this was the beginning of the end for both of them. Deep down inside I felt sad for them because the death of a relationship is always hard on the individual involved; it is a really painful experience for whoever goes through it. In my experience, many people end up turning their back on God because they blame Him for the failure of their relationship; for the fact that they could not make their relationship work. I was worried that one of them would leave the Church and maybe even leave their faith. When I heard that the engagement was off and they had broken up again, I knew that this time it was over for good and that they had no chance of getting back together again. The young man eventually left the church because of His heartbreak; it was a traumatic experience for Him. Daysi continued in the church but also with a broken heart. I did my best to remain a good and supporting friend to her during this period, to be there for her whenever she needed me and console her during those moments she broke down.

It was true that they had broken up but I did not jump up at that. I had learned through my various experiences and disappointments that things were not always the way they appeared, God works in incredible ways and His ways are a mystery to us at times. I did not presume to know it at that moment, I had given up on that struggle; I was just focused on Him, on our relationship. I was no longer demanding or trying to force things to work, I had learnt that the hard way. You should learn from this to never try to force anything on God, no, instead, let Him work at His own pace, let Him control and work things in His own way, any other thing would be identical to wasting of time. See, God always answers our prayer, the problem becomes when we don't like the answer. His answers are simple and direct. God either tells you to let go (**NO**), he tells you it's yours (**Yes**), or he tells you, not yet (**Wait**).

Reflection

Questions for Chapter 9

Answer the following questions taken from this section, and focus your mind

Write down your answers and thoughts

1. Name a time when something has gone your way and you felt undeserving of it.

_____

_____

_____

_____

_____

_____

_____

_____

_____

_____

_____

2. What is something God said no to you about, and how did he show it?

_____

_____

_____

_____

_____
_____
_____
_____
_____
_____

3. What is something God said yes to you about, and
how did he show it?

_____
_____
_____
_____
_____
_____
_____
_____
_____
_____
_____

4. What is something God said wait to you about and
how did he show it?

_____
_____
_____
_____
_____
_____
_____

Victor Armando Martinez

Chapter 10

All In

I still had feelings for Daysi, I had not really gotten over how I felt about her but I chose to wait for a while and exercise patience before I made my move.

I was not interested in getting her on a rebound from her last relationship. I told myself that I would wait for at least 2 months before I let her know that I liked her, I would let her get over her ex-fiancé and grief over the loss of that relationship before I tried to get into her life. In my mind, I felt that she liked me already but

113

was too scared to say anything. I started thinking that she was hiding her feelings for me. Boy was I wrong!

I thought that when I confessed my love to her, that she would confess her love for me as well. I had deceived myself into thinking that my catching feelings for her would be shared, that all the times of being close to her and being friends must have resulted in her developing feelings for me as well.

The day that I confessed my love to her finally came two months later.

The day was sunny and beautiful, yet a little chilly. The wind was still and yet could be heard in the trees above. I drove Daysi home with my younger sister after church in my blue beat up 1992 Ford F-150. I remember it like yesterday. I didn't talk much in the 30-minute drive across town. I kept rehearsing what I would say to her over and over in my head, my heart beating faster as we got closer to her house.

I stopped the truck in front of her house, got out and opened the door, helped her out the truck and continued to walk her to her door. I hoped for the best but still, just in case, prepared myself for the worst.

As we walked up the steps of her porch, I could hear my heart beat louder and louder; a sign of nervousness.

My heart raced faster and faster as she reached for her door handle. In my head, I could hear her confessing that she had feelings for me too. The moment of truth came...

"*Daysi I want to tell you something,*" I said as she was about to push the door open. She turned and looked at me waiting for what I wanted to say. I blurted out, "*Daysi I like you, and would like to get to know you more.*"

She responded quickly with confidence and assurance. I expected her to say something along the lines of, "*I just see you as a friend.*" or "*I'm in love with you.*"

But she looked at me instead and said, "*I can't tell you 'no' or 'yes', just pray about it.*"

She then turned and walked into her house. Yea, not exactly what I expected...

As I walked back to my truck, all I could think of in my head was, "*She didn't say NO.*"

I smiled the whole way home. In fact, all I could think of was the TV show *Family Matters*, with the characters *Steve Urkel* and *Laura Winslow*. The show revolved around the fact that *Urkel* was madly in love with *Laura*, who did not return his love. Anytime she would treat him nice he would say, "*I'm wearing you down, Baby.*" And by the end of the series, he had gotten his girl.

The next three months were filled with attempt upon attempt to try and make *Daysi* my girlfriend, but they all failed. Every time I would ask her to be my girlfriend, her answer would always be the same, "*Just pray about it,*" to which I would reply, "*Ok I will.*"

It had become like a song. In my mind, I was wearing her down and breaking down her defences and barriers. However, in reality, she was turning me down repeatedly, I just did not know it or maybe I did not want to see and acknowledge it.

I decided to take out all the stops and go all out for her. Since Daysi did not have a car of her own, I decided to buy one for her; the best that I could afford.

I purchased a **2003 BMW Z4** two seater for her. It was the most beautiful car I had ever purchased. I told her that I wanted to help her since she did not have a car and assured her that there were no hidden motives. I know, I know. Devious, right?

I brought it to her on a Friday evening after church. I parked the car in front of the church so that she could see it and be amazed as she came out of the church. She was very surprised, she then told me, *"**Can you bring it to me tomorrow at the park?**"*

Her family would be having a family picnic on that day.

I took the car to the park the following day and as I approached where *Daysi* was I felt in my body that something was off. I parked the car and walked down to where she was seated. I noticed that she was serious and a bit detached from the event that was going on. As I got to the pavilion, she turned and told me, **"I am not taking the car."**

I asked her why she was refusing it but she would not respond.

I walked away disappointed, upset and hurt. I raced out of the park as fast as I could to show my frustration. It did not work.

"Why would she mislead me?" I asked myself. But then again: I had been misleading her. I knew that I got what I deserved.

I did not stop asking her to be my girlfriend though. Then one day I got a call from her at home which quite surprised and excited me as she had never given me a call at home before.

I quickly ran out of the apartment so no one would hear me. As we started to talk, I tried to think of a clear reason why she would call.

"She must just be calling to ask me some unimportant question," I told myself.

But then, the call turned to 10 and, then to 20 minutes. It then dawned on me that she just wanted to talk to me. Her reason for calling was just to hear my voice and converse with me.

More than two hours later I realized that this could actually happen; I could actually get her to be my girlfriend. I enjoyed every minute of our conversation together. Even though the whole time I was standing in a dirty cold laundry room at the apartment we lived in with nothing but socks on my feet, on solid concrete, I enjoyed every moment of it.

As *Daysi* and I continued to grow in our relationship in the following weeks and months, my mom began to catch on to my intentions for her and she was not excited about it at all. The issue was that Daysi could not express her feelings very well; she did not wear her feeling on her sleeves at all. Daysi seldom communicated how she felt. As if things could get any worse, my recently turned 18-year-old younger sister disappeared with who we all assumed was Daysi's younger brother. This sparked a war with my family.

My sister hadn't come home for days and we were all worried sick about her as we had no idea what could have happened to her. We suspected that Daysi's younger brother had taken and hidden her in their mother's house and as the oldest in the house, I took charge of looking for her.

The day after she had disappeared I called Daysi, who lived in the same house as her brother. I thought that if she knew where my sister was she would tell me.

But no luck, "***No se (don't know)***", was what Daysi told me. I felt somehow that she was lying to me and I got upset with her.

I called her again that same day to convince her to tell me the truth. This time Daysi told me that my sister is afraid of me. Daysi began picturing me as an abusive person. She began asking me if I easily got angry. At this point, I was shocked and surprised at what I was hearing. I began to feel my chances with Daysi disintegrating with every word.

I felt upset and deeply betrayed by the accusations in her voice and I abruptly told her, *"You can think whatever you want"*, after which I hung up the phone.

I told myself that I would ask her to date me just one last time and that if she does not say yes, I would leave her alone and go my way, I told myself, **"I am better than this."**

Monday came around and I decided to make my last and final move. I called up Daysi and asked her if I could bring lunch over to where she was. She agreed. I brought her a *Chipotle Burrito*, which I knew she liked as she had already told me some time before. I drove over to Cub foods to buy her a flower and when I got there, I could not get a single flower so I bought a bouquet of roses for her instead.

The bouquet seemed a bit of overkill, and I did not want my gesture to appear extravagant. So I took one of the flowers and placed it inside the lunch bag. Then, while I walked back to my car, I noticed a short middle-aged woman coming towards me. I stopped and said to her, *"Hello, would you like these flowers?"* She looked at me and gave me a huge smile and I handed her the rest of the bouquet of flowers.

As I drove into the parking lot of the place where Daysi worked. I thought to myself, **"This is it, my last stand, my last attempt."** I prepared myself for the worst which could not be more than a refusal to have anything to do with me and then I headed in.

As I entered into the office, I found *Daysi* already waiting for me. She turned towards me and I gave her the lunch I brought for her. She opened the lunch bag and was pleasantly surprised when she saw the flower I had placed inside.

"*Will you be my girlfriend?*" I finally blurted out and *Daysi*, with a smile on her face, responded and said:

"*Ok, you can tell people*".

To which I replied, "*Ok.*"

I then turned around and walked back to my car.

When I got back to where I parked, I entered and sat in my car for a while. I could not believe that I really experienced what I just did; it felt dreamlike and unreal, I thought to myself:

"*What had just happened?*"

I picked up my phone and put a call through to *Daysi* on her work phone to clarify what just happened.

"*Hello, Daysi,*" I said.

"*Yes?*" she responded.

"*Does this mean we're dating?*" I asked.

To which she responded: "*Yes.*"

I then said: "*Thank you, bye*", after which I hung up.

Yes I know. Comical, right?

After that, I sent text messages to a number of church members. The message was simple, clear and straightforward.

"*Daysi and I are now dating.*" And by that evening, the whole church knew about us. Nine months down the line after her saying "**yes**" to me, we got married in church and then, nine months after our wedding, we bought a beautiful house and had our first child.

I had finally gotten my dream girl; a girl that checked off all the items on my list. God had finally come through for me in the most miraculous and unexpected way. He kept His word and fulfilled His promise.

After my searching far and wide for a woman, unknowingly to me, he had placed her under my nose from the very beginning. The woman of my dreams had been right in front of my eyes the whole time, at arm's length from me. I did not need to go through all the struggles and stress that I did. All I had to do was to trust Him and let Him work in His time and in His own way. I should have just had faith in Him and be patient with Him and he would eventually have come through for me like he did. He proved Himself mightier than my rantings and ravings, he proved Himself as a Father who really, truly, cares and is always working towards achieving and accomplishing my dreams and goals for me.

Using this story as a background, I will outline how exactly you can put yourself in a position to not only get the woman/man of your dreams, but to ask and get all your heart's desires in **Chapter 16**.

After the wait, the heartbreaks, the rejections, he gave me the desires of my heart, like the father in the story who had a dealership, I gave Him the specifications of the woman I wanted and he gave her to me. He actualized my dream. Daysi was everything I requested for, and she had the physical, spiritual and mental attributes that I desired. We cannot know when or in what form, but we should be steadfast in our faith in Him because sooner or later, he will accomplish our heart's desires for us. He is definitely working towards our fulfilment.

"Until now you have not asked [the Father] for anything in my name; but now ask and keep on asking and you will receive, so that your joy may be full and complete."

John 16:24 (AMP)

Like the old saying goes, *"the proof is in the pudding"*, this means that you can only judge the truth of something after you have tried and experienced it yourself.

The pudding was over 10 years in the making. My faith had developed stronger than ever before. I now saw how real God can be in our life if we truly trust in Him. I had been struggling with my finances and love life. I had lived in a dysfunctional home, always moving around and sometimes even being homeless for my whole life.

However, by the age of 25, I had the woman of my dreams, beautiful home, beautiful family, and I began to prosper in my finances all in the next 12 months. I felt as if God had opened the windows of heaven and had blessed me abundantly, all because I trusted Him.

Ask yourself, do you think your dreams and heart's desires are worth your obedience? Do you want to live a life that few dare to live? A life of peace, joy, and hope. The odds are that it won't be easy for you; not because God requires us to jump through hoops, but because he requires us to trust Him.

And I will do whatever you ask in My name [a]as My representative], this I will do, so that the Father may be glorified and celebrated in the Son. If you ask Me anything in My name [as My representative], I will do it

John 14:13-14 (AMP)

Why does God want to give us the desires of our heart? Simple: As God seeks to bless and build a strong relationship with us, he goes out of his way for us to love and seek him. What better way to cultivate this relationship then to be our ultimate Provider of all our needs, and everything we truly want.

If you don't believe me read this:

He who did not spare [even] His own Son, but gave Him up for us all, how will He not also, along with Him, graciously give us all things?

123

Romans 8:32 (AMP)

You see, if God was so willing to give his own son to sinners like us, what else would he **NOT** do for us? His desire is for us and he will do everything in his power to show us that.

Reflection

Questions for Chapter 10

Answer the following questions taken from this section, and focus your mind

Write down your answers and thoughts

1. Reflecting on your life, which desires has God already given you?

_____

_____

_____

_____

_____

_____

_____

_____

_____

_____

_____

2. List some new desires you have?

_____

_____

_____

_____

_____

_____

_____

_____

_____

_____

_____

_____

3. What does God have to do in your heart to get you
   ready for your hearts desires?

_____

_____

_____

_____

_____

_____

_____

_____

_____

_____

_____

_____

_____

Chapter 11

My story of how God brought me the man of my dreams: My husband.

By Daysi Penaloza Martinez

My name is Daysi Penaloza Martinez. I married Victor on May 7th, 2011. Little did I know that God would use my new husband to give me the desires of my heart; desires that I didn't even know I had.

I came from an even more dysfunctional and chaotic background than my husband. I don't even know where I was born in Mexico. All I know is that I was given away as a little girl to a wealthy family on the west coast of Guerrero Mexico, all because my mother could not provide for our family.

My new family was emotionally, physically and sexually abusive to me. One time my adopted mother got me so drunk that she threw me into the ocean to watch me struggle, simply to amuse herself.

I remember meeting my real mother for the first time when I was 10 years old. I felt like a princess being rescued from the wicked family when my stepdad and older brother came to take me back home.

Life with my real family was peaceful even though we lived in poverty. I was happy that the abuse had stopped.

A few years later my mother made the decision to come to the United States with the hopes of sending us back money to feed us. At age 14, I made the decision to come to the States to be able to save money for myself. I didn't know God was orchestrating the biggest miracle of my life and that somebody was praying for me long before I knew it.

I met Victor at a church my family began attending in 2006. I had reluctantly agreed to accompany them to the church one day. The people at the church were so nice and the Pastor showed a real love for the people. My first year in the church was life-changing, I had accepted Jesus into my heart and I found myself excited to know God more. Victor was one of the young adults at the Church; he also seemed very active in every area of the Ministry.

The 1st year I was at the church, I began dating a boy I had known before my time at the church. He was a nice person and I thought I would be happy with him. Shortly after we began dating, he proposed marriage and we set a date. I was a new Christian during this time; I did not know the Bible very well, but as I read and studied it, God would speak into my life in a powerful and beautiful way.

I had multiple experiences with God that deepened my relationship with Him even more. The closer I got to God, the more I began to feel uneasy about the man I was engaged to marry. I felt like a veil was being lifted off my eyes. I no longer felt peace in my heart and I began to ask God to give me wisdom. As the wedding date neared, a desire began to grow in me and I made the decision to serve God for the rest of my life. I realized that I did not want to make the mistake of getting married and then getting divorced later.

The Lord in His mercy began to show me things that would hurt me in the future. I saw a future in which I was unhappily married, I saw myself sad, depressed, and very lonely. The future with this man began to look like a huge mistake waiting to happen.

Then one day the Lord gave me a prophetic word, he told me that if I did not listen to him, and disobeyed, the future would be very bad for me because the person I was with was not for me.

After praying for a few days, I decided to end the engagement and the relationship. I decided to believe God for His promise that he had something better for me. It was very hard for me to break it off with him because so many people knew of our plans and I had made so many new friends that would be disappointed with me. But the Lord had given me the wisdom and courage to leave all of that. I decided to take steps to the future and not look back.

My friendship with Victor was a weird one. As he and I began to work closely with the youth ministry, we would often bump heads. Once I told the Pastor that Victor kept arguing with me. He quickly brought us into the office and told Victor to stop fighting with me. I felt like all he wanted to do was argue.

As time passed, Victor would often give me advice about life, which really helped me understand many things. Our friendship grew closer and closer because of it, but only as good friends. I never felt attracted to him at all.

Months after my break up, Victor confessed his feelings for me. I could not bear hurting anybody's feelings, so all I could say to him was to pray about it. I just saw him as a friend.

I remember spending weeks on my knees in prayer in my room. My prayer was simple and direct:

*"**God give me my husband, give me a man who loves and serves you.**"*

During this time, I had not heard of the list of which Victor talks about in this book, and I wasn't sure about everything I wanted in my husband.

*"**I do have a couple of must-haves,**"* I told the Lord.

I asked God that I wanted my husband's parents to be from *Guadalajara* or the *Jalisco* state of *Mexico*, and I wanted him to be born in California. I also wanted him to be a sociable person and a go-getter; a person that was not lazy and knew how to get things done. I thought of a man who didn't take long to make decisions and was quick on his feet. I wanted him to be of a light complexion as well.

During these weeks of prayer, I had little to no knowledge of Victor's family and/or their background. I had told God that my husband could be any man, just not Victor. I just didn't feel any attraction to him. I was set on my decision, and I even had other guys in mind for God to choose from.

Everything changed one night when I had a very intense dream. In this dream, I saw a man hugging me, and I had an overwhelming feeling of sincere love, protection and an amazing sense of peace. I had never experienced such strong feelings in my life before. As I pulled away from the man hugging me I saw his face, and to my surprise, it was Victor!

I quickly woke up in desperation and said: *"**No, no puede ser possible (no, no it can't be)!**"*

131

Quickly God answered me in the most powerful way possible; I heard the audible voice of God! He said:

"WHY NOT VICTOR, WHY NOT VICTOR, WHY NOT VICTOR?"

He had repeated Himself three times, he not only wanted my attention but he wanted to correct my heart. At that very moment, a supernatural birth took place inside of me; it was a deep love and affection for Victor. I had never felt any desire for Victor before, all of sudden I had a strong sense of wanting to be with him. The next day I picked up my phone and called Victor just to say hi for the first time (I had never called him before). Our conversation quickly turned into hours of conversation about nothing really, I just had a deep desire to get to know him more.

After that day, I looked forward to seeing Victor every chance I could get. Every time I saw him, I got excited and felt happy. My affection and love for him grew and grew by the day.

Now during this whole time, Victor kept asking me to be his girlfriend, to which I kept telling him to pray about it. I still wanted to take my time to be sure he was the one. I eventually told him yes after a few weeks of him asking. Several months after dating, Victor and I became engaged. Nine months later, we got married, and the rest is history. We now have a very happy family with three beautiful children. Victor and I have only grown more and more in love with every year that goes by.

This journey confirmed to me that God is interested in our desires and that he is great enough to move mountains to bless us. If God could supernaturally change my heart, he can do the impossible for you. God loves our sincere heart; he yearns to hear our prayers.

Make today the decision to seek Him and follow His way, it will be more than worth it. As time passed, I learned to trust God for more of my heart's desires. I know that my prayers are only limited by my obedience and faith, but I face the future, which is filled with His promises, and I don't look back.

Reflection

Questions for Chapter 11

Answer the following questions taken from this section, and focus your mind

Write down your answers and thoughts

1. How has God used someone else to give you the desires of your heart?

_____

_____

_____

_____

_____

_____

_____

_____

_____

_____

_____

_____

2. What kind of lies hinder a person from coming to God for help and direction?

_____

_____

_____

_____

_____

_____

_____

_____

_____

_____

_____

_____

3. What past experiences hold you back from walking with God?

_____

_____

_____

_____

_____

_____

_____

_____

_____

_____

_____

_____

_____

_____

_____

_____

_____

_____

_____

_____

_____

_____

_____

Chapter 12

Hindsight: Why did it take so long?

Google defines hindsight as an understanding of a situation or event only after it has happened or developed. The amazing part of hindsight is that since God is all-knowing he already knows what will happen and why. Only time lets a man see what God was seeing the whole time that we were going through something.

Don't get me wrong: sometimes people get hurt. Sometimes horrible things happen to good, well-meaning people, but it is not because God wanted it that way. Most of the time it's man that messes up the good things that God has for us.

God is constantly working on our mistakes and our disobedience to work things out for His own children that do obey and act with selflessness. God's divine plan is to perfect us for Himself. He wants us to have a heart like His. A heart of love, compassion and obedience, and this is not just for Gods glory but it's for our own good. He does not want us to wallow in sin and destruction. He wants to rescue us.

God isn't complicated, we are. I don't presume to say that we will understand everything that happens in our life here on earth, but one day we will understand. That day will be in heaven when we will come face to face with God Himself. However, until that happens we will ask God for wisdom and discernment to understand our situation and make sense of what is going on around us. We must fight against pride, selfishness and rebelliousness, for those are the things that hinder our ability to see what God is doing in our lives.

A few months into my marriage, my eyes were open. I felt like God Himself took the blindfold off my face and I realized why God took so long to give her to me. I wasn't ready:

When I turned 23, I began to tell God that I would take my dream girl even if she weren't ready for me. I told God that I would deal with the consequences of not waiting any longer....

Boy, was that a mistake! I thank God that he did not listen to my impatient and stubborn words. The issue was not just that God was working on her. He was working on me! I assumed the whole time that I was ready for marriage, ready for that next step in my life. I was wrong. Not only was she not ready, but I still had a huge issue controlling my own emotions.

Although I was not violent, I did wear my emotions too much on my sleeve. This was not a good thing. Years of being raised with screams and shouts twisted my idea of effective communication. Instead of me being a steady rock to give my family a foundation, I too often became emotional and wanted things my way. As you can see this was a disaster waiting to happen.

So how did I realize I was not ready? Simple: marriage brought me face to face with my selfishness. I suppressed and hid it as best I could, but it kept coming back every day. I tried thinking positive and godly thoughts, and it didn't work. The problem was immaturity. I was not mature enough. I didn't know how and when to express my feelings.

When I realized this I said to myself, *"If you're 25 now and can barely handle your emotions, I can't imagine how you would have been if you were married at 20."*

I perfectly understood why God had me wait. Until he could trust me with His beautiful daughter, I would not have her.

Most people don't know how to steward or properly handle what they already have, whether it's management of their finances, marriage or children, most people are often unwilling to cultivate what God has given them, they just look elsewhere for a better deal. Yet people always want more. People think by having more they will be happier and more fulfilled because they feel they can finally have enough for their needs. The Bible speaks to this very clearly.

Whoever can be trusted with very little can also be trusted with much, and whoever is dishonest with very little will also be dishonest with much. So if you have not been trustworthy in handling worldly wealth, who will trust you with true riches? And if you have not been trustworthy with someone else's property, who will give you property of your own? See **Luke 16:10-12 (NIV)**

Daysi and I Conquer our Money

When I first made my contract with God at 16 years old, I noted on there that I wanted to prosper financially. I wanted to have more than enough. I had lived in poverty my whole life up to that point and I didn't want that lifestyle to follow me.

I knew I needed help since everyone that my family knew wasn't really well-off either. The few people that we did know that lived ok would never give us financial advice... or perhaps they didn't even know how to.

I struggled with my finances for the first few years as an adult. I assumed that as I grew up I would naturally become financially better off, I didn't. I began to get frustrated in my twenties until I came back to God's word and began to ask for Wisdom to manage my finances. I acknowledged I needed help.

Since I was 20 years of age I made over **$40,000** a year with no college diploma. I thought I was making good money. I thought I was going to have my own place with a new car and money to spend on whatever I wanted. But the truth was: I was struggling. I had roommates and I couldn't pay my rent on time. I had a beat-up truck that was sucking up gas and costing a lot in repairs.

I thought my solution was to work harder. This caused a lot of frustration and at times depression in me. I didn't let God teach me how to be a good Stewart with what I already had.

When I couldn't pay my bills and I couldn't faithfully give to my church I didn't ask God to give me a new Job with more money. I asked Him to help me control my spending urges and to teach me. I knew I had a problem spending my money. I knew that I had to control and keep a budget before I got married. I didn't want to go into a marriage mismanaging my money.

Six months before I got married I made my prayer. *"God give me the Wisdom to control my money"*. I chose to rely on Gods Wisdom and provision. Daysi and I entered our marriage broke, I had $1 to my name on the night of our honeymoon.

I wasn't discouraged, I knew God would turn it around, I kept asking for Wisdom and I learned to give generously to the work of the gospel. Two years later, we were able to pay off my student loan debt, buy our dream home, buy a newer car, have my wife stay home for Six months raising our daughter, and give over $20,000 in charity.

This was the beginning of God giving my wife and I our hearts' desires as a couple. God wasn't done yet. *Daysi* and I began to trust God for even more. Even with our income now combined at almost **$70,000** we still were struggling to save and manage our bills. We continued to believe God for the Wisdom to manage our money. I wanted to accumulate wealth for our family. I asked God to prosper us and to give us more. Since God saw we could handle and honour Him with a **$70,000** family income he opened more doors and our family started making almost **$100.000** a year (this was amazing since I only had 1 year of college education and my wife had none).

The issue still was that we could not accumulate a savings or investments. *"**God prosper us, teach me**"* I prayed again. This time we were able to invest into my 401k over **$30,000** in 3 years and save over **$20,000** in our HSA savings account. God was giving us our hearts desires.

When we ask for our hearts desires, remember God wants to give us what we want, but more than that, he wants us to become what he wants. He wants us to have a heart that reflects His. He wants us to let Him work in our lives for His glory and for our own good. Many times we already have what we want, a wife, family, money and so forth, we just simply need to ask God to teach us how to cultivate what we already have for it to become what we really want. Why does God make us wait? He is either working on us, or he is working in someone else.

If most people were not willing to handle and steward what they already have, why would God give them more? Let God give you the Wisdom to nurture what you have and it will grow into all you want.

Reflection

Questions for Chapter 12

Answer the following questions taken from this section, and focus your mind

Write down your answers and thoughts

1. What lessons have you learned from making hasty and emotional decisions in the past?

_____

_____

_____

_____

_____

_____

_____

_____

_____

_____

_____

_____

2. List some of your heart's desires that you have so far.

_____

_____

_____

_____

_____

_____

_____

_____

_____

_____

_____

_____

_____

_____

3. List one thing that you will wait on God for.

_____

_____

_____

_____

_____

_____

_____

_____

_____

_____

Chapter 13

Three who dared

I know that the process that I went through to get all I wanted in my Dream Girl was long, rough and hard. I know that it was difficult and anxious with many challenges. This was my journey; remember I started this journey when I was just 16 years of age.

Maybe you will start your own journey much older than that, or you might be much younger but know that everyone's story is and will be different.

Amidst the differences can be found some fundamental truths about the word of God which if followed faithfully will bring blessings you may have never expected. These truths which if we live our lives by them and make them a guideline will lead to a wonderful and fulfilling life. I did not say a perfect life, no, I cannot promise that. What I can say and promise though is that if you follow His truths and live by them, you will have lived a life so wonderful that only a few have had the pleasure and privilege to live.

That person is like a tree planted by streams of water, which yields its fruit in season and whose leaf does not wither, whatever they do, prospers.

Psalm 1:3 (NIV)

I want to tell you the story of three people who dared to believe God for all they wanted in their dream girl/guy as I had, who dared to put their affairs in His hands and what happened to them. I gave two of the three the framework found in this book, they followed it to the letter and they got exactly what they wanted as they had planned it and believed God for. The third person is a personal story shared by **Josh Clintwood**; he shares his story in his own words of how God brought his dream girl, *Morgan*, into his life.

Max's Story:

Meet *Max* (not his real name). He was one of the best men at my wedding. I had known *Max* for a long time, about 5 years as at that time. *Max* was my wingman and we were quite close. He was a young man in the youth group that was under my care in church. I personally mentored and discipled him. He soon worked with me in the youth ministry. *Max* had a front row seat to the story that was my life. *Max* saw and witnessed my entire journey. He saw the wait, he saw the struggle and he saw the victory.

Soon it was *Max*'s turn to seek the woman of his dreams. He started out believing that God would actually give him the desires of his heart and so therefore, I gave him the recipe to follow (this recipe is in chapter 16).

He took this recipe and I could tell he brushed it off in his heart. As the weeks turned into months and things did not seem to be moving fast enough as he wanted, he began to lose faith. He would pursue girls that were not interested in him. He would chase after women that were not really his type, much like I had done during my own journey.

His confidence began to fail and he started to lose faith in himself. As I noticed the abysmal process he was in and the downward path he seemed to be on, I stepped in and advised him, telling Him: "***Learn from my mistakes, build your list and stick to it***" I would say.

The list began with one, two, three items which were quite vague and not detailed or specific enough. He would ask for, 1- a girl 2- speaks Spanish and so on.

I challenged him. I told him that if he really trusts God, he would make a real list and that he would avoid many heartaches that way. After that talk, he got more serious with the list and it began to grow, the items got more specific: white woman with blue eyes, educated, loves food just like me (yes, he liked food), and she must love *Latino* culture. When he showed me, I said "**you got it**."

Now it was time to wait and have faith, trust the list and trust that God loves you enough to actualize it. I told him to relax and leave the reins in God's hands and watch Him perform His wonders.

A year later, we parted ways due to ministry changes and I did not see him until over a year after that. The next time I saw him he had big news for me. He was going to get married, God had come through for him too, and his dedication, patience and tolerance had finally yielded encouraging results. Guess to whom he was getting married? The Girl of his dreams, the girl he had asked for and planned for in his list. She was the desire of his heart.

Merissa's Story:

And then, there is *Merissa* (not her real name), she was my neighbor. She was a Godly single woman who always seemed busy traveling. She became good friends with my wife and I.

Merissa was in her early thirties when she told my wife and I that she was ready to find the man of her dreams and settle down. I told her about my adventure to get my dream girl who at that time had become my wife. She was hooked immediately and instantly fell in love with the idea of trusting God for exactly what she wanted.

She started her list which was also initially vague, short and not specific enough:

1- Must be a Christian;
2-Must be sweet; and so on.

When I noticed this, I challenged her to be specific and detail what she wanted but she did not know what else she wanted apart from these. As she began to date men her list quickly grew when she was able to pinpoint what she wanted and did not want. It is a funny thing that some people have to see what they do not want before they realize what they do want. Often, time reveals what we truly need. You might even realize what you get is really what you wanted the whole time.

Finally, the list was solid; it was complete with every detail and specifics she wanted. She added height requirements and specific personality traits, she added every single attribute that interested her and that she wished for in her dream man. Nine months later, God brought him to her and within a year, they were joined together in marriage. Now they are a beautiful family of four with two awesome children.

Josh Clintwood's Story:

Growing up, my dad always told me that the two most important decisions I would make in my life was, first, whether or not I'd accept the call to follow Jesus, and, second, who I chose to marry. I took these two decisions very seriously. When I was young, I would pray for my future wife. I would pray that God would keep her safe and that he would mould her into the uniquely gifted woman that He made her to be.

Throughout high school I never dated or sought out a relationship, trusting that God would lead me into the right relationship at the right time. God had begun shaping my identity and my view on dating. The more I found myself seeking God, the more I began to develop my list of qualities to look for in my future wife. However, at this point, I didn't have an actual list, but more so had a broad idea of the wife I was looking for.

When I graduated high school in 2012, I moved from Illinois to Minnesota to attend a small Bible College in Minneapolis, MN. Within the first week of being there, I found myself sitting in a large circle of freshman students. Stereotypically, Bible colleges are known by their *"ring by spring"* culture. The students in the circle were describing what would be their *"dream"* spouse.

A lot of these lists were ultra-specific and lacked realistic qualities. Before it was my turn, I took a step back to really consider what I desired in my future spouse, beyond strange specific preferences. This is the list I came up with:

1. She would have a genuine faith in Jesus, beyond Sunday mornings, that is interwoven with every aspect of her life.

2. She would be culturally aware of those around her, as well as her own identity and background.

3. She would be creative and enjoy creating in some capacity.

4. She would be adventurous and spontaneous and open to trying new things.

5. She would be cheap and thrifty, being a good steward of the resources God has given her.

As I walked away from the circle, I didn't plan on finding that *"dream"* girl anytime soon. As many of my newly met guy friends talked about wanting to get married by sophomore year, I was really content with waiting however long God wanted me to wait. At this point in my life, I was more concerned with growing in my relationship with God than pursuing a romantic relationship.

The following week, as classes started, I was put in a pre-assigned group in one of my classes where I met a girl named *Morgan* from Minneapolis. Since I was new to the city, I was trying to connect with anyone that was local.

I got her number, as did everyone in our group, with no intentions of pursuing her beyond using her as my personal yellow pages. Besides, there wasn't any initial attraction and I wasn't really interested in dating a white girl. God would later break down this barrier of mine.

A couple of my friends wanted to bike around the city, so I asked *Morgan* if she would want to show us around. We had about five people who were going to come. At the last minute everyone cancelled, except *Morgan* and me. Since there was no interest in going out one on one, we rescheduled for the next night. Strangely enough, everyone cancelled at the last minute again. We decided to go ahead and bike around together. During that night, we learned that we shared a lot of similar passions and perspectives on faith, people, and culture. We both ended that night, feeling that we had just met a really good friend. Over the next two months, *Morgan* continued to show me around the city. Through the places we explored and the conversations we had, God slowly revealed to me that my list of qualities for a "**dream**" spouse perfectly described *Morgan*.

As I saw these qualities in her, God began forming a deep love within me for her, and I began to pursue a relationship with her. Fast forward, we have been married since May 2014, have a son named Marquelle and co-run a media company together.

If you truly seek God, He will give you the desires of your heart, as ***Psalms 37:4-5 (KJV)*** beautifully describes:

> *Take delight in the Lord, and he will give you the*
> *desires of your heart. Commit your way to the Lord;*
> *trust in him and he will do this*

As we grow in Christ, we are able to discern between desires that are in line with God, and desires that can be hurtful and damaging to not only our life but also our relationship with Him. He truly knows what we need to walk in the steps he has planned before us. I could not have dreamt up a perfect spouse for me, and the qualities in *Morgan* go beyond my initial list. *Morgan* is not perfect, and neither am I, but the gift of our marriage has been a taste of God's sacrificial love and abundant grace.

Victor Armando Martinez

If you trust in God and work according to His framework, then he would definitely grant your desires. If your faith stands strong and you dare to trust in Him, you dare to believe in Him to accomplish your desires and deliver to you (in this case) your dream man/woman then he definitely will, all you need to do is exercise your faith. The list is not magic. It is simply your words in action. A declaration of faith and purpose that commits you to trusting God. A clear way to define your wants and desires with God. God is not a genie that is there to grant you your wish. There is a framework that must be followed in order to be in the position to ask from Him whatever you want.

Reflection

Questions for Chapter 13

Answer the following questions taken from this section, and focus your mind

Write down your answers and thoughts

1. How can you identify with these stories?

_____

_____

_____

_____

_____

_____

_____

_____

_____

_____

_____

_____

2. What are some ways in which peoples' testimonies help us?

_____

_____

_____

_____

_____
_____
_____
_____
_____
_____
_____
_____
_____

3. Who around you can you seek out for motivation?

_____
_____
_____
_____
_____
_____
_____
_____
_____
_____
_____
_____
_____

Chapter 14

Don't Misunderstand

If you have read this far, the biggest mistake you can make is thinking that getting exactly what you want from God means smooth sailing and no issues. You could think it means that you would not have any problems because it does not mean that at all. Another mistake we can make is thinking that everything we want will come to pass. We need to understand that some of the best things that could happen to us never do.

There are going to be bumps, bruises, and plain mess-ups in your marriage or in anything you get that you have always wanted. There will be disagreements, challenges and maybe arguments. Sometimes not getting what we want turns out to be the biggest blessing. Nevertheless, the key is to trust that God will wade in and smooth everything over for His glory and our own good.

Marriage was hard for us the first year. We got into arguments all the time, people at church thought we had the perfect marriage, but it was far from that, we had our own internal issues. We had problems so big that at a particular point in our marriage we were planning to split and go our separate ways. Yes, we were contemplating divorce.

Things were not going the way I expected it to go. I had envisioned a marriage that would be smooth and pleasurable right through. I would often tell God:

"Lord, I don't understand what is going on but I am going to hold on a little longer, and as long as you don't let go, I won't either."

This prayer often came with tears and agony as it was made in pain.

Someone once said that if you want to be like Jesus get married. Marriage is a lifelong commitment of continuous forgiveness, just like Jesus always forgives us we learn to forgive our spouse. See, marriage causes you to trust God, it causes you understand Christ more and to become more like Christ, to be closer to Him. I would often tell God: "teach me your ways, show me what to do and how to go."

The lessons usually came through patience and waiting for Him to work things out in my heart or in the heart of my wife. Marriage is hard, but nothing worth having is easy. When God gives you more, it often requires more responsibility from you. As God gives us the desires of our hearts, he will require more from us.

> *"…From everyone who has been given much, much will be demanded; and from the one who has been entrusted with much, much more will be asked."*
>
> *Luke 12:48 (NIV)*

Tired and worn out after six months of fighting I wanted to give up our marriage, it was not the paradise I had envisioned; we were constantly bickering and disagreeing over one thing or the other. I finally conceded to a divorce that Daysi had been asking for. I did not want to fight for our marriage anymore, I was ready to give up and throw everything away. However, we waited a little longer before the final decision. Little did we know that God in His mercy was working on us, on our pride, on our rebelliousness, on everything, he was helping us smooth over our issues. He was forging us into one and helping us understand each other more.

"...but those who hope in the LORD will renew their strength. They will soar on wings like eagles; they will run and not grow weary, they will walk and not be faint."

Isaiah 40:31 (NIV)

While it would have been extremely easy to just give up and walk away from our marriage we didn't, we persevered, we knew that God did not plan on divorces in marriage, everything God does is perfect and if he brought us together, we would achieve a growing and blessed marriage.

We were both contemplating divorce because we were suffering in our marriage but then, we understood that divorce was not the solution we were looking for. We trusted God to work things out and iron out the kinks for us, I, my wife and God were in our relationship, and with His help, eventually, we got over our problems and have come to love each other more and more over time. I am constantly surprised at how our marriage keeps getting better though the years. God has been more than good.

I have told you these things, that my joy and delight may be in you, and that your joy and gladness may be of full measure and complete and overflowing

John 15:11 (AMPC)

This is to tell you and show you that no marriage or God given desire is safe from problems and that even after getting that (dream desire) dream man or woman that you have dreamed about, planned and prayed for, problems still arise. Instead of throwing in the towel and giving up, call on God, he will work things out for you if you just hold on and trust Him. Pray to Him and communicate with your partner while working on yourself and on your relationship.

Situations will arise when your spouse will wrong you and when they do, be like Christ, forgive and do not let hate and hurt fester in your heart. Forgive and let go of the hurt. See your spouse as your equal and someone who you are supposed to work together with, trust each other completely and reveal each other's thoughts. Even though the husband is the head of the house and the woman should be submissive, they are both partners in marriage, both of you should be closer than any other person should, you should be best friends. There are many passages in the bible that point to these truths. In *Genesis 2:24*, God says:

"That is why a man leaves his father and mother and be joined to his wife. And the two people will become one."

This same passage is repeated in the bible in *Matt 19:5* and *Eph 5:31*

This is to impress upon you the fact that both of you should be tight and very close; you should be each other's best friends and confidants; you should be as **ONE**.

And in everything you do, put God first, consult Him, seek His opinion, let Him lead and direct you and in no time, you will enjoy pleasure like no other. Things and desires in themselves don't make anyone happy all the time. We will mature and often our desires will change. Only God can truly make us happy. We will always find joy and pleasure in what we have, as long as we ask God to give us the joy we seek.

Sometimes we won't feel fulfilment when God finally gives us what we wanted. It is not the final outcome that truly makes us happy. It is the fact that we are connected to the one who created us and longs to be with us that should bring fulfilment to us. This fact shouldn't shock us because as we mature in our faith, our relationship with God will be so rich that he will be all you really desire. He is the Blesser that gives the blessings. He is the source of where the water comes from. People can leave and enter your life but God will never leave you. The Bible tells us that no one can separate us from His love. He is the answer to our desires. He is all we really want. That is what heaven will be like. He will provide for all our needs and truly make us happy and fulfilled in the very thing we do. Heaven is our true home where our father will lavish us with His love and presence for eternity. We will be His and he will be ours, to love forever.

May the God of hope fill you with all joy and peace in believing [through the experience of your faith] that by the power of the Holy Spirit you will abound in hope and overflow with confidence in His promises.

Romans 15:13 (AMP)

Reflection

Questions for Chapter 14

Answer the following questions taken from this section, and focus your mind

Write down your answers and thoughts

1. What are some of the toughest and most sincere prayers you have prayed?

_____

_____

_____

_____

_____

_____

_____

_____

_____

_____

_____

_____

_____

2. How would a close relationship with God benefit your desires?

_____

_____

_____

_____

_____

_____

_____

_____

_____

_____

_____

3. Why aren't some people unwilling to pursue God for their desires?

_____

_____

_____

_____

_____

_____

_____

_____

_____

_____

_____

Chapter 15

I Found My Father

I never knew about my father growing up. I never even wondered about Him. I guess you don't miss what you never had...

When I saw other families with a father, I just thought that they were somehow lucky and blessed. Never did it occur to me that I wanted a father, at least not until I got into high school. In high school, a hunger and desire began to be birthed in me. A hunger and desire for a father. I was becoming a young man, but I did not

170

know how to become a confident young man. I ignored that hunger for a few years, not knowing what to do about it. Little did I know that God in His love and mercy would grant another desire of my heart, one that I truly wanted, but was afraid to ask for. I truly believe Gods word when it says:

Ask and you shall receive, seek and you shall find, ask and you shall receive"

Matthew 7:7 (NIV)

There is power when our faith turns into action when we are able to vocalize our desires to God. I understood this principle early on in my life.

However, I never thought about asking God for me not only to meet my biological father but also to have a relationship with him. I had a hole in my life that needed to be filled. That hole was a desire to know my father; to know where I came from.

Up until this time, I had heard multiple stories of my father, ranging from him being involved in a car crash and becoming disabled, telling my mom to leave him since he wouldn't be able to provide any longer, to him being a drug dealer that crossed the border often with special cargo.

None of it made sense. My curiosity began to boil, and one day when I was about 14 years old, I asked my mother the name of my father. She hesitated for a while and finally told me, his name is Armando Barajas.

Moreover, for the next 10 years she never spoke his name again.

In my early twenties, I attended a church that began to offer these spiritual inner healing retreats. They were composed of three full and intense days of biblical teaching and prayer. The topics touched on a ton of different areas of our life, from forgiveness, health and diet, abuse and so forth.

It was during the "*inner healing*" session that the Holy Spirit highlighted and exposed an area of my heart that I had forgotten about and needed to address.

The Pastor talked about the lack of love from the absence of a father that many people have experienced. He related his own experience with his own father, and of the hatred, he had for him, when he witnessed his younger brother being brutally punished by him. He eventually came to forgiving and loving his father again.

When he talked about how some of us never met our father, I began to cry uncontrollably. I did not understand why I cried.

As the years passed by, our church would host these retreats every few months. I would eventually become a helper and listen to the same sermons about inner healing over and over... and every single time the Pastor would talk about the lack of a father, I would cry. However, by this time my eyes would just water like two faucets that had major leaks.

After about 5 years of these retreats, the unexpected happened to me: As I stood at the back of the room, again balling, the Pastor Looked at me with eyes of compassion and said to me: *"quieres conocer a tu papa" (do you want to meet your father)?"*

I stood there, somewhat ashamed to admit to anyone that I had been crying because I did not know my father. I nodded my head, thinking that was the end of it.

Then the Pastor said: *"Dile que quieres conocerlo" (tell him you want to meet him)"*.

I looked at the Pastor as he waited for me to vocalize my prayer. I felt an eternity passed as he waited for me to answer, the pressure mounting as everyone was staring at me.

I felt fear, a sense of selfishness and unbelief that God would grant me such a request. I surrendered to my desire and said: *"Senor quiero conocer a mi papa" (Lord I want to know my father.)"*

I remember a strong sense of doubt, but still, inside I felt like God heard me.

The following year was full of failed attempts to get my mom and her side of the family to tell me who my father was. My mom would not budge and my family swore they did not know who he was. I knew that if I were to find out, I would need to fly to Mexico and find him myself. Three years later, my wife and I would take the trip deep down in Mexico to unravel a secret twenty-eight years in the making. Armed with nothing but faith that God heard me 4 years earlier, and that he would grant me the desires of my heart.

In **2015**, my wife and I landed in *Puerto Vallarta, Mexico* for a short vacation, three days later we took a bus to *Guadalajara* to meet my grandma, aunts, and uncles that I had not seen in over 20 years. Deep down inside I knew that my family new more about my father then they let on. I felt a strong sense that I would find my father. After two days in Mexico connecting to my family roots, I put my faith into action. I began to take certain members of my extended family to the side and ask questions. My mom quickly got wind of it and was furious. She had my relatives threaten not to say anything about my father. I shook it off and knew God would bless me with my heart's desire. I told myself that even if my dad did not want me, I would at least find closure, but deep down inside I wanted my father in my life.

By the third day, my Grandma and aunt realized that I would not stop until I found my father. My *Mama Lupe* (maternal grandmother) would take me on a secret mission to talk to an old family friend that still lived in the old neighbourhood where she raised my mom. She would take me to the corner of Juan Valdivia and Jose Fernandez, but to no avail, the trail went cold quick.

That evening I went to my aunt Maricela's house. Her and my mom were two peas in a pod growing up, they did everything together.

"**She must know something**", I said to myself.

However, she would not talk. As I made another plea to her I began to cry. I begged her to tell me, and with the help of my cousins she did, *"no se quien es tu papa pero si se quien puede saver donde vive (I do not know who your dad is but I know who might know where he lives)."*

Off we went, on another secret mission, only to land back at the corner of Juan Valdivia and Jose Fernandez. We knocked at what I could assume was the neighborhood busy body. She was not home.

My Aunt quickly said, *"Nemodos" (o well we tried)."*

However, I stood strong, I grabbed on to the promise God gave me, to give me the desires of my heart.

"There is no cause more noble and more just than mine," I said as I reminded God of my request.

Remember, by now God had given me the woman of my list, my dream girl, dream home, and the wisdom to accumulate wealth. My faith was at an all-time high. I knew I would find my father, even if I had to knock on every door in the neighbourhood asking for *Armando Barajas*.

I told my aunt, *"volla tocar cada puerta aqui (I will knock on every door here). Vamos a comiensar con esta (let us start with this one)."*

I turned around to face the first door closest to me.

"Ting ting!" my Aunt hit the tin bars with a peso she had in her pocket.

Soon a woman came out to meet us at the front gate.

*"**Estamos buscando Armando Barajas (we are looking for Armando Barajas)."*** my Aunt said.

*"**Quien lo busca?" (Who is looking for him?)**,"* the Lady asked.

As I heard those words, I felt my body become light, and my breathing slowed down so as not to miss the next words. We had found him on the first knock! I felt amazed that God would move so quickly. The woman turned out to be *Patricia*, the wife of my dad's brother Hugo.

I would learn that my father was arrested a few years earlier. He was in the *State Prison*. The adventure was not over: it had just begun. I found out that my dad had other children, two of which lived nearby.

That evening my dad's brother Hugo took me to see my sisters. However, to avoid any potential issues with my dad's ex-wife, my uncle had me pretend that I was my dad's brother. I did not feel comfortable lying but I was in shock the whole time, not knowing what to say. I felt like a ghost listening to every word around me, hoping to memorize every step and face I saw.

When I saw my blood sister *Fernanda* for the first time, I felt an amazing connection to her. *Fernanda* was 13 and my other biological sister *Angela* was 7 years old. I saw some of my facial features on her. It was a powerful moment. I remember staring at their faces, doing my best to memorize every feature about them. That evening we made a game plan to visit our father that Sunday.

Sunday morning arrived on a beautiful and clear-sky day. My Uncle Hugo and I picked up my sisters *Fernanda, Angela* and their older sister *Diana*. I soon found out that the jails in *Guadalajara* were very different from the ones in the States. The jails there looked more like a huge picnic area. We were able to bring food, sit, and talk on picnic tables for hours.

As we cleared security, I felt my heart race, my body somewhat numb and my breathing slowing down as not to disrupt anything around me. During the security screening, I was separated from my Uncle and sisters.

I was first in an area that I call *"**The Park**"*; I gave my dad's name to one of the inmates waiting at the entrance. He quickly ran to go look for him. It was super weird for me. I did not see any police officers in the park, everything there was ran by the inmates themselves. They were helping the visitors with anything they could, hoping to get a tip for their service. They even had restaurants with waiters attending to the people's needs. It was an amazing experience.

My uncle and sisters soon entered, and together we sat at a picnic table waiting for our father. I felt jittery and nervous, gazing out at the multitude of people.

My sisters began to notice my odd behaviour. I decided to tell them the truth, as I turned to them.

I said: *"**Armando Barajas es mi papa, (Armando Barajas is my father)**."*

My sister *Fernanda*'s face lit up with excitement. She would later tell me that she had a hunch I was his son all along. No one knew what to say next. We just waited.

As we sat, my sister *Fernanda* jumped up and ran to whom I figured was our father. I stood up to greet him as formally as I possibly could, trying my best to make a great first impression. I stuck out my hand to give him a firm handshake. I stared at him with what I could only guess was an intense stare.

"*I look like him*," I told myself as we sat down to talk. I was surprised at how composed I was. I had a billion questions to ask him, but all I could do was stare at him.

"*He is a handsome man*," I thought to myself; he had a full thick set of black and grey hair, his face well-defined with colourful eyes, his shoulders well defined and a deep yet soft voice that made him sound wise.

"*I have good genes*," I said to myself.

The conversation quickly turned awkward as my dad told me my birthday, which happened to be the wrong month, date and year. I quickly corrected him with the correct dates, which was one year sooner than his. To my surprise, he stood his ground and he again uttered the same month, date and year. I again corrected him with my actual birthday.

As we stared at each other, we both realized that he was talking about another son, also named *Victor*! Yes, I had a younger brother named *Victor*, and the whole time my father assumed I was him! My father then tells me that he did not know I existed; he was more shocked than I was.

What a revelation, my father never had the chance to pursue a relationship with me because he did not know I existed. This new information somehow comforted me. I was free to start a relationship with him without the thought of *"being unwanted"* over my head.

As my time with him ended, I did not feel anything I assumed I was going to feel. No high emotional rollercoaster, pain or desire to cry. In my head, I planned that I was going to give him some words of encouragement and pray with him as we parted ways.

Boy was I wrong! As soon as I stood up to excuse myself, a powerful feeling that I had never felt before came over me. I began to shake and cry uncontrollably, trying my best to speak the words of encouragement that I had planned on saying. I felt like a giant baby, I could not speak or move right. Every step I took felt like a challenge. I remember shaking as he walked me to the main entrance of the park, doing my best to breathe and not to trip over myself in the process. I hugged him one more time wishing never to lose him again.

I felt a new desire born in me; a desire to love and share my life with my father. I made a decision that I would let God use me to love and be a light to my dad's side of the family. I desired to know everything about my new family, including finding my long-lost siblings.

As I let him go, I walked out of the park, constantly looking back. He just stood there looking at me, which in turn made me cry even more. It felt like a scene out of a movie. It felt so surreal. I could not believe how God would grant me this desire. I felt so privileged to have had this opportunity.

The next two years would be full of acceptance and love from every member of my dad's family. I got to meet my paternal Grandmother *Esperanza* (Mama Gaby) in California along with my only Aunt and her children, which were all amazing.

My Cousin Marcos looked like a taller version of myself; it was a little awkward at first, but super cool. I would also meet and hit it off with my Grandfather Armando Barajas Moreno (He had separated from my grandmother over 40 years earlier and had another family).

My father and most of his siblings hand not spoken to him in over twenty years. My Grandfather would use me to send them his love and open arms. Little did I realize that God would be using me to build a bridge in my father's family. My eyes widened, and I felt an amazing feeling of accomplishment and privilege because I knew that only God could work this out so well for me. My new hope and desire are to allow God to continue to use me to bring my paternal family together for His glory and our good.

In this chapter, I want us to realize that we all have desires. Many times, we let our low self-image or past heartbreaks stop us from dreaming and asking God for what we really want. Sometimes we do not feel worthy of asking for fear that people will judge or make fun of our desire.

In my case, I even had family opposing and stopping me from realizing and pursuing my desire. My mom was very angry with me at first but as time went by, she was ok with me getting to know my dad's side of the family.

Remember, God Himself has placed the desires you have within you. If God is on your side who should you fear?

If God is for us, who can be against us?

Romans 8:31 (NIV)

Trust Him; seek His direction in your life.

Proverbs 3:6 tells us that God will make our path straight if we submit to Him. When you submit to the Creator of the Universe you will find yourself with an even closer relationship with God Himself, and closer to your dreams!

A young man once told me that he was satisfied with just knowing God was with him. He did not need to talk to Him every day or build his relationship with Him he said.

I felt sadness in my heart I knew inside of me that he would be giving up so much more than just a closer relationship with God; that he would lose wisdom and guidance to help Him manoeuvre around unnecessary landmines that he would for sure encounter over the course of his life. God wants to be your confidant, your support, and your Light. Turn to Him for help; talk to Him, he will listen, and he will act on your behalf.

The Lord will fight for you; you need only to be still

Exodus 14:14 (NIV)

Imagine having God work out your path for you, making it straight and making your burden lighter.

Take my yoke upon you and learn from me, for I am gentle and humble in heart, and you will find rest for your souls. For my yoke is easy and my burden is light."

Matthew 11:30 (NIV)

Meditate on God's word, seek Him, and he will show you desires you didn't even know you had. Don't settle for mediocracy, dare to live the life you desire. Do not let fear or peoples' judgments hold you back from having **ALL YOU WANT**.

Reflection

Questions for Chapter 15

Answer the following questions taken from this section, and focus your mind

Write down your answers and thoughts

1. What is a desire you have that you can't bring yourself to verbalize?

_____

_____

_____

_____

_____

_____

_____

_____

_____

_____

_____

2. How does fear hold us back from our hearts desires?

_____

_____

_____

_____

_____

_____

_____

_____

_____

3. What needs to happen in order for us to break
through our fears?

_____

_____

_____

_____

_____

_____

_____

_____

_____

_____

_____

_____

Chapter 16

The Frame-Work

I want to illustrate Gods framework as easy and as simple as possible. In order to be in a position to ask God for your desires and wants, you have to work together all the key parts. Applying one without the other will not work but will cause confusion and unnecessary frustration.

Faith is the gas, the framework is the vehicle and seeking godly Wisdom is your smartphone that helps you figure out where you are, together they guide you to your hearts desires. Remember God is not complicated, he doesn't confuse us, we are the complicated ones, so don't complicate it! Some People may think that's its harder then I make it sound, all I have to say to those people is that they need to get out of their own way.

Faith   **Framework**   **Godly wisdom**

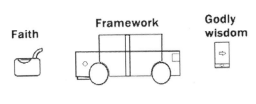

Faith is the gas that moves everything. The framework is the vehicle that will take you where you and God want to go. The smartphone is the wisdom needed to fill in the blanks of how to get to those desires as quick and as smooth as possible. Once all these parts are working together, you are ready to ASK FOR WHAT YOU WANT!

Do not be anxious or worried about anything, but in everything [every circumstance and situation] by prayer and petition with thanksgiving, continue to make your [specific] requests known to God.

Philippians 4:6 (AMP)

Step 1. The Architect

Believe in Jesus Christ. (It's His framework)

The first and most important step is to realize that God, in His love and mercy, set a plan for our own good. That plan was designed to cultivate a relationship directly between man and God Himself. God designed even the very desires of man. Since the beginning, God gave man free will to choose to do evil or good. God's plan is to bless and prosper man, to fulfil man's desire.

For I know the plans I have for you," declares the Lord, "plans to prosper you and not to harm you, plans to give you hope and a future.

Jeremiah 29:11 (NIV)

God is the greatest architect and designer that has ever existed. Not only did he design the whole Universe but he designed every integral part of man. Some people see man as cattle whose sole purpose is to live and die. Others see man's relationship with God as nothing more than a creator and His creation, nothing more. As you have read in All You Want, God wants to be much more involved in our lives. He designed us with desires, consecrated them to be fulfilled in our very lives.

I once read a story of a man whose car had broken down on the side of the road (this was when the first model T cars were being massed produced in America). Along came another man and desired to help the stranded man. They popped the hood, and within seconds the helping man had the vehicle up in running. Who was this man? Henry Ford. You see, since Henry Ford designed and build the model T car, he knew how to get it working properly.

This is the exact situation we find ourselves with God. He is the creator and designer of our very own desires. He knows exactly how to fulfil them in our lives. His framework is set up just for this. To give us our desires. If you truly want all the things your heart desire, you must believe in His plan and redemption for your life. If you find your life in a rut, unfulfilled, not motivated or simply going from bad to worse, stop and change directions right now.

Step 2. Intimacy

Fall in love with Jesus

Honesty + *Transparency* + *Dependency* =<u>Intimacy</u>

Some people may read this book and think that I am making God out to be some sort of candy machine. Where if you push the right button and make the right payment you get what you want. That couldn't be further from the truth. Intimacy with God is what will actually separate those who simply see God as a means and those who see further than just their physical wants, but also see their spiritual desires. God doesn't give us our desires simply because we behave and say that we believe in Him. Intimacy takes time and effort to build.

God created marriage to show us the type of relationship he wanted with humanity. Marriage was God's way of drawing a parallel for us. You see, what makes marriage different from other types of relationships is intimacy. Intimacy is what makes our marriage fulfilling and connected; it's what makes it work. This is the same with our relationship with God. We will only be able to enjoy God's full blessings if we chose to become intimate with Him. How do I build intimacy with God you ask? The principles are actually the same way you build intimacy in your marriage.

The foundation of your relationship with God should rest on:

1- Honesty

Google defines honest as — free of deceit and untruthfulness; sincere. Our feelings and intentions with God must be honest. See, even though God knows our hearts and thoughts, he still wants us to approach Him with a straightforward heart. Some of us may come with doubts, shame, fears, and anger, yet God wants to hear how you feel with your own mouth. He is not surprised by our words and feelings. We must understand that God feels just like we feel, he hurts like we hurt, he understands why we feel the way we do (**John 11:35**). Do not let your feelings hold you back from approaching Him with what is in your heart. This is what the Bible means when it says to come as we are (**Revelation 22:17**). Often in our marriages, the absence of honesty leads to cracks and eventually disillusionment. Yet in order for a marriage to survive, there must be a restart of honesty. If you have walked away from God, come back to Him, and tell Him how you feel.

2- Transparency

Google defines transparent as "easy to perceive or detect". As Americans, this one will be harder to accomplish. We live in a culture full of pride, arrogance and know it all. We avoid being perceived that we don't have everything under control or that we need help. We always try to show a façade of strength and power so as not to attract pity even when we do actually need help. We must put down our pride and acknowledge that we don't know everything and that we cannot do it alone.

Since the fall of Adam and Eve humanity has been fractured and broken. Sin, pain, and sickness have run rampant in our world. Sooner or later we let sin creep into our own lives and families, it moves in our homes like carbon dioxide, unable to be detected unless we have equipped our homes with the ability to alert us of it. When sin enters our lives and families, it brings death and destruction. The only way to be redeemed from our sin and death is through our connection with God.

> *(he) made us alive with Christ even when we were dead in transgressions--it is by grace you have been saved"*
>
> **Ephesians 2:5 (NIV)**

This is what I mean by transparency. We have to be transparent with God. No one is perfect and we all need to be redeemed. We lose our favor and connection with God the moment we think we no longer need to depend and seek God's direction in our lives. This principle holds true in marriage and family as well. When we no longer think we need each other, we begin to implode. Our children see that mom and dad no longer acknowledge each other, they see the lack of respect and transparency in the family which eventually brings destruction to the whole family unit in the end.

3- Dependency

Google defines dependence as "the state of relying on or being controlled by someone or something else. Very powerful words right? This may scare away some people; especially those who are well off or find themselves in a good season in their life. Nobody likes to be dependent on anyone else. They think to themselves that dependency means tied down and limited. We assume that being dependant on God will somehow take away from our life. We tend to believe that if we are dependent on God, then he will use and possibly take advantage of us. This is not true at all. Listen to what Jesus says to His people;

How often I have longed to gather your children together, as a hen gathers her chicks under her wings, and you were not willing.

Matthew 23:37 (NIV)

Let's think about it, our children are dependent on us as parents to stay safe, the husband and wife depend on each other to cultivate love at home, and we are dependent on authority to run a smooth society. Dependence is not a scary thing when administered by a loving, righteous and caring authority. The Bible tells us that God is love and that he has great plans for our lives. Do not see dependency on God as a burden, but see it as an asset, someone whom we can depend and rely on always. Someone that will love us and seek us, even when we don't deserve it. He becomes our strength and encouragement. No matter how strong you think you are, you will need Him.

Even youths grow tired and weary, and young men stumble and fall; but those who hope in the Lord will renew their strength. They will soar on wings like eagles; they will run and not grow weary, they will walk and not be faint.

Isaiah 40:30-31 (NIV)

As you can see, building an intimate relationship with God is not easy. But nothing **worth having** is easily obtainable. A great marriage isn't easy, it takes time and work. Intimacy takes time and work. It is not something you can easily rush to develop. No matter how hard we work we need to understand that as we build intimacy with God, we become more in tune with His work in our lives. We begin to discern and feel what God is doing in us and through us. I heard once, that people would not mind going through tough situations in life if we knew why we were going through it in the first place. Intimacy takes us on the amazing journey, one that not only will show us how to find favor with God but one that will show us the heart of God for us. His love is great, and everything he does is to bring us to a closer and more personal relationship with Him.

Step 3. The Rules

Let God's word guide you.

Let them be what you live your life by. Obedience is not a bad thing, it is a privilege.

Have you ever wondered what to do in a situation, found it hard to make a decision, or maybe you were not sure what to think of an event in your life? These questions have challenged and hunted every person that has ever been born. Allowing the right thoughts to consume your mind are extremely important in order to make the right decisions at the right time. Earlier in All You Want, I explained that we needed to be desperate for Wisdom and that we should constantly be asking God for more of it. The first place every person should look for is God's word. Remember, King

Solomon wrote and shared the Wisdom given to Him by God in the book of Proverbs. The Bible also tells us the following;

All scripture is given by inspiration of God, and is profitable for doctrine, for reproof, for correction, for instruction in righteousness: That the man of God may be perfect, thoroughly furnished unto all good works.

2 Timothy 3:16-17 (KJV)

The whole Bible is there to teach us and guide us. The bible gives teachings and advice about the most frequent issues and situations that have ever faced humankind. The odds of the Bible speaking of your particular situation is very high. The only issue is finding where to find the answer, but with the advancements of technology, all we need to do is ask Google, "What does the bible says about…." then we have our answer. On complicated matters, we have Pastors, who can assist with further clarification if Google, Siri or Alexa becomes biased or unhelpful in their responses. The amazing thing about having the word of God available to us is that it gives us the ability to filter any advice given to us, even if it is from a Pastor or Priest or any other religious Leader. With so many people making themselves out to be the final authority on matters, we need to depend more on the word of God to test if the advice given does line up with the word of God. Resist the urge to put in higher esteem those who speak eloquently or persuasively, even if they call themselves Christians. I once heard a

Pastor advice a woman member of his church to leave her husband if he did not want to come to church with her. This is an example of advice that is contrary to the word of God. The woman should not have listened. The Bible says the following on unbelieving husbands;

To the rest I say this (I, not the Lord): If any brother has a wife who is not a believer and she is willing to live with him, he must not divorce her. And if a woman has a husband who is not a believer and he is willing to live with her, she must not divorce him. For the unbelieving husband has been sanctified through his wife, and the unbelieving wife has been sanctified through her believing husband...

1 Corinthians 7:12-14 (NIV)

I also had a man tell me once that he learned from His Priest that he does not have to talk to God every day; he told Him that he just had to know God is with Him. This again is contrary to the word of God. The bible says the following;

...but in every situation, by prayer and petition, with thanksgiving, present your requests to God.

Philippians 4:6 (NIV)

We must always be talking to God, it is not because he does not know what we want, but because he wants to have a relationship with us, and that only happens with communication. The Bible reinforces this truth many times: here is another verse for example;

And pray in the Spirit on all occasions with all kinds of prayers and requests. With this in mind, be alert and always keep on praying for all the Lord's people.

Ephesians 6:18 (NIV)

I can go on and on about what the bible says on all types of issues. Everything from depression, anxiety, death, financial management (yes money, the Bible talks more about money than it does salvation), how to treat people and so on. All of us have questions, and the word of God can answer them.

The Bible has withstood the test of time and the world's greatest critics, it is the number 1 selling book ever written and has given hope and encouragement to Millions of people. Few doubt the reliable nature of the Bible. It is Gods ordained word that guides and brings hope to everyone, listen to it.

Step 4. Time to Soar

Understand that as your faith rises, you will intimidate people around you, they will follow you or they will resist and judge you, which will only mean one thing, you are going to have to let them go. Often critics will say, "You have changed". To which you should respond, "You're darn right, I do want to better myself". Do not be intimidated by them.

If you have not been scared off with these challenging steps by now, this might do it for you. Maybe you are thinking in your head, *"No-one can do these."* Well, you're wrong. I did, and many others before me and many more after me will as well.

Remember, God is not asking us to be perfect. He is simply asking us to learn to trust Him, which takes time. The only thing that makes these steps so challenging is the fact that most of your friends and family will not understand or be willing to encourage you on this adventure. In fact, not only will they not be there for you, they will often begin to feel challenged and threatened by your developing faith. Most people think they do not need anyone, they think they can figure it out themselves. They do not want anyone to tell them what to do or how to do it. You have to understand that your faith will separate you from many of your friends that want to settle for less.

I remember many times feeling like an outsider: I felt I did not belong. I remember telling myself that I wanted all the blessings I had heard in God's word, and I assumed that everyone else wanted them also.

In high school, I had a friend name, Boris. He was a Russian kid adopted by white parents. At adoption, they changed his name to Matt, to sound more Americanized.

Matt struggled with depression, drugs, sex, schizophrenia and a loss of identity. I would often tell Matt about how Jesus loved him and that he could take away all those things from him. Matt sounded interested but did not want to attend a youth service with me. I continued inviting him and finally one day, I told him to try everything he wanted to find peace but if it did not work, he should try Jesus.

He looked at me and agreed. Three weeks later he approached me and said: "*I am ready to try Jesus*".

That week I took him to our youth group where my younger brother Joel was preaching. The message was about how we needed God and how God could take away our sins and give us the peace we seek. Matt raised his hand to receive Jesus in his life at that moment. He cried as he repeated the words inviting Jesus into his life.

When the youth service was over he turned to me still crying and said," *I feel like all the voices have stopped*". I told him, that is what Jesus can do for you.

The next 3 weeks were filled with a new joy and peace in Boris' life. He decided to embrace his Russian background and go by his biological name.

Then one day, it all came crashing down. As I sat in the cafeteria with Boris one day he looked different; he looked down again and said he was struggling to follow Jesus. His family had begun to disqualify what was going on in his life. They told him he did not need Jesus, and Boris listened.

Boris then told me, "*If you want to be my friend, don't talk to me about Jesus anymore.*"

Everyone wants a better life, everyone wants joy, peace and all the blessings that come with having a relationship with Jesus, but few are willing to confront the critics that try to make you feel less. Run from them; delete their number from your phone if you have to. We cannot ask for our heart's desire without having a close and intimate relationship with God, and if people get in the way of that relationship you must cut them off. The process is not easy, but extremely worth it. God will shock and surprise you with the blessings he wants to give you; it is greater than your wildest dreams.

Heaven is the ultimate reward

I want to say one more thing in this section. Many critics would say, *"what about all the Christians who are suffering in the world, or the desires that some people never get in this life, should they have faith? And if so, are they not holy enough? Is their relationship with God not valid? What if, instead of their desires, they get pain and death?"*

I am not ignorant of the fact that many Christians have given their life for the cause of Christ in the mission fields. I understand that there are godly people all over the world that face hardships and disasters because of their faith, where are their desires? When do they get their hearts' desires met? For this answer, we must again go back to the Word of God, because it gives us the answer.

Jesus said, "I assure you and most solemnly say to you, there is no one who has given up a house or brothers or sisters or mother or father or children or farms, for My sake and for the gospel's sake, who will not receive a hundred times as much now in the present age—houses and brothers and sisters and mothers and children and farms—along with persecutions; and in the age to come, eternal life. But many who are first will be last, and the last, first."

Mark 10:29-31 (MSG)

Jesus is very well aware of the fact that many will face pain, destruction and evil for His name's sake. Jesus gives us hope; he tells us that those who go through such tribulation will be rewarded in heaven! As we read deeper into the subject we read;

I saw thrones on which were seated those who had been given authority to judge. And I saw the souls of those who had been beheaded because of their testimony about Jesus and because of the word of God. They came to life and reigned with Christ a thousand years

Revelation 20:4 (NIV)

Jesus has prepared a special place in heaven, for those who have suffered for Christ sake. They will be rewarded accordingly. But what of those who are not martyred yet live in poverty and constantly lack basic resources? Again, the Bible gives us answers and hopes as well. It says;

But without faith it is impossible to [walk with God and] please Him, for whoever comes [near] to God must [necessarily] believe that God exists and that He rewards those who [earnestly and diligently] seek Him.

Hebrews 11:6 (NIV)

In heaven, there are rewards waiting for those who choose an intimate relationship with Christ. You will have your desires; you will have your dreams sooner or later.

Step 5. Pop Quizzes

Your resolve will always be tested, the higher the blessings the higher the tests that you will undergo. Keep standing in your faith, be determined and you will triumph in the end.

What is it that separates those who begin this adventure and reach their God-given desires and those who do not? It is simply the patients and obedience to endure trials and test. Everyone is tested and everyone goes through trials. Some people chose to resent God and walk away from Him because of those trials, others chose to feel sorry for themselves and settle, and very few dare to trust God in the midst of pain and discouragement. It is important to see what the Bible says about this process:

And not only this, but [with joy] let us glory in our sufferings and rejoice in our hardships, knowing that hardship (distress, pressure, trouble) produces patient endurance; and endurance, proven character (spiritual maturity); and proven character, hope and confident assurance [of eternal salvation]. Such hope [in God's promises] never disappoints us, because God's love has been abundantly poured out within our hearts through the Holy Spirit who was given to us.

Romans 5:3-6 (AMP)

In other words: hardship produces patience, patience produces endurance, endurance produces a proven character (spiritual maturity), and spiritual maturity gives us hope and confidence in our loving God who gives us the promise of heaven.

The bible shines a positive light on trials and tests; it says that the main purpose of trails is to develop our relationship with God and His promises. Someone once said that we would not mind going through trials and struggles as long as we knew why we were going through them in the first place. Now we know. God is always working on our character. Nobody likes not being in control. However, Gods main goal is to give you the things your heart truly wants and desires. As that old television program says, "**Father knows bes**t".

Our Godly father knows best.

Very few people let this process take effect. It is a never-ending process where in God is preparing us for the glory to come, here on earth and eventually in heaven. We must have the belief that God is in control of everything and that he has nothing but good things in store for us. The Bible also says:

> *And we know that all things work together for good to them that love God, to them who are the called according to His purpose.*
>
> *Romans 8:28 (KJV)*

God is constantly using the struggles to develop our character as a godly person. He wants us to trust Him with everything we have. God often targets our biggest weakness. Maybe your weakness is a self-reliance on yourself. That means he will target and test the things you feel that you can do without Him. God wants us to understand the following:

> *And to the angel (divine messenger) of the church in [a] Philadelphia write: "... He who opens and no one will [be able to] shut, and He who shuts and no one opens:*

Revelation 3:7-8 (AMP)

He is the one that has the keys to your blessings. He is the one who opens the doors for you and me. Let us learn to trust Him in everything we do.

If your weakness is obedience's he will target your sins, we must discipline our lives in order to preserve our homes, family, business, and future. We all know that it only takes one big sin to bring it all down, and we all know that the big sins start out small. God knows this and wants us to obey His will in our lives, let go, and Him. The peace and joy this truth brings changes everything for the better. God's plans are for good in our life. We cannot choose His framework and at the same time ignore His calls for us to repent of our sins and transgressions. Some of us hold hate, resentment, envy, malice and all sorts of other evils in our heart. Little do we know that those same sins that we hold onto can eventually cost us everything. Jesus said it best:

"Why do you call Me 'Lord, Lord,' and do not practice what I tell you?

Luke 6:46 (AMP)

As we mature and grow in our intimacy with God we will be tested at every new level. As I have said before, "to him much is given much will be required". The more you get the more God will challenge you to give away, whether its money, influence or anything else of value you have. Do not make the error many make. The more people get the less they tend to give. The challenges are real, God is always watching, and God is always rooting for you.

Step 6 - #1

Be careful never to replace the Blesser with the blessings. Always keep your relationship with **God as your #1 priority**.

We need to ask ourselves, *"Who is our number one priority"*? Most Christians would say their family, marriage, and other righteous options are their number one priority. However, very few would say God. In addition, if they do say God, others will classify you as extremist, weirdos, and other things not so pleasant.

The problem is that most people fail to understand that God is our biggest cheerleader, coach, and referee. Can you imagine a sports player that does not care about his fans, does not follow his coach's direction and who does not respect the referees? Crazy right? You see, God wants to move heaven and earth for us! Imagine that!

Yet so many people start to move him down on the personal totem pole once they begin to accomplish and accumulate the desires of their heart. I personally have seen this happen repeatedly in people's lives. They think it is best to follow their own ideas and opinions, then to follow the creator of the Universe and His word for our life. Crazy right?

How do you know if God is really the number one priority in your life? Easy. All you need to do is find what your treasure is, what do you value above everything else? The way we figure this out is with a simple formula.

Where do you put your extra?

Money + Time + Energy = <u>your treasure/your top priority</u>

Money

How do we calculate money? Easy. The first and easiest way is to pull your bank statement and calculate where your extra money is going. Are you giving financially to your church, ministry or missionary (Gods work) regularly? Or do u prefer to go out to eat, travel or buy new things instead?

Some people may say that they do not have extra money to give because their mortgage, car, and credit card payments are too high. Once we see this, then we know their treasure is their home and possessions. This type of person sees the accumulation of "**things**" as their **#1 priority/ treasure**. They subscribe to the notion that whoever dies with the most toys, wins.

Others may say that they do not give regularly to Gods work because they want their kids in all sorts of extracurricular activities, a special private school, and/or other family activities. This might sound righteous at first; however, as one looks further, one would discover that such a person's kids are their idols.

Please don't misunderstand: I want my kids to have the best as well, but never at the expense of bringing God down from His position as **Number One**. Remember God is the One who blessed us by giving us the kids; the blessings in our family will come from Him. We need his protection for our family every day.

Time

Do you attend Church on a regular basis? Is your family involved in ministry on regular bases? Or, do you prefer to spend time with your friends, sports, working out or just sleeping in?

Once again, don't get me wrong: I am not saying that those things are bad; what I am saying is where we put our extra time is a clear indication of where our treasure is. We must understand that our treasure becomes our idol. If we are more interested in ourselves then we become the *"number one"* at the top of the totem pole.

Energy

What do you spend your time thinking about, what do you constantly find yourself planning or worrying about? Your thoughts take a ton of energy. Do you meditate on God and His role in your life? Do you let Gods word examine and correct your heart? Before you act, do you ask God for guidance for advice? Most people do not, but if you have read this far, you are one of those people that does want God to be part of your daily life, you do want to walk in His way, you do believe that God does want to give you the desires of your heart.

If we could understand that the good things we have are all because God has given them to us, then this point will be easy to understand. However, if you feel like it's all up to you to make things happen it will be much harder to realize that you need **God as your #1 priority**. This mind-set makes us become prideful and self-reliant, eventually causing us to miss the mark. The problem is that most people begin to make their success, comfort, and other people their main priority.

Step 7. Slow and steady

Remember it is a marathon, not a race. Slow and steady living wins the race. Do not be in haste, have patience and **go-it-gently**.

People's eyes light up when I share with them the amazing plan God has for us and how His desire is to give us our desires. There are 4 types of responses once the initial excitement passes.

The following are the responses I usually get from people once I share these truths. Jesus illustrates these responses very well when he says:

Then he told them many things in parables, saying: "A farmer went out to sow his seed. As he was scattering the seed, some fell along the path, and the birds came and ate it up. Some fell on rocky places, where it did not have much soil. It sprang up quickly, because the soil was shallow. But when the sun came up, the plants were scorched, and they withered because they had no root. 7 Other seed fell among thorns, which grew up and choked the plants. Still other seed fell on good soil, where it produced a crop—a hundred, sixty or thirty times what was sown.

Matthew 13:3-8 (NIV)

The seeds that where ate by the birds once they fell on the path are the people that pause in wonderful amazement, thinking to themselves, *"Can it really be true?"* However, immediately after they pop out of those wonderful thoughts and hopes, they quickly return to a look of unbelief and doubt.

Next, we have the seeds that withered away on the rock. They did not have much soil and sprouted quickly. The roots could not go deeper to survive because the soil was shallow. These, are the people who were excited for a few days, but when it became time to make the list of their desires and hopes, they soon found that they are too busy to make the list and eventually forgot all about it. Their dreams were exactly that... just dreams.

The thorns that eventually killed the seeds that grew up are those who make their list and wait, only to succumb to temptation and youthful impulses that cause them to settle for a lot less than they hoped.

The seeds that fell on good soil are those who push through and put all their hope in God's framework, eventually getting all their desires fulfilled. Their faith and perseverance inspire others around them to believe Gods plan and framework for their own life.

The key to persevere to the end is **discipline**. The *Apostle Paul* summed it up perfectly:

> *Therefore I do not run like someone running aimlessly; I do not fight like a boxer beating the air. No, I strike a blow to my body and make it my slave so that after I have preached to others, I myself will not be disqualified for the prize.*
>
> *1 Corinthians 9:26-27 (NIV)*

Paul is telling us that we must subdue our body, thoughts, and spirit. We must learn to control what we think and how we behave.

Self-control is the only way to reach **ALL YOU WANT**.

How do we subdue our body? With the same intensity that an athlete trains his body. Be impatient and do not give up. Trust the process and Gods word. Celebrate the small victories as they come. Find a way to inspire and raise your faith. Talk to Godly people for advice and direction, look for a trainer and counsellor or mentor to help cheer you on. Address your impatience with strategy and tenacity. Getting all you want is not easy but it is definitely worth the process.

God's framework can apply to all areas of your life. You see, when you follow and put yourself in a position to obey and follow Jesus, you put yourself in a position of blessings. Understand that your desires and request can only be submitted to God if you really believe and are willing to let God work it out for you. I never thought I could have the desires of my heart growing up in poverty and in a broken home. But as I wrote down my hearts desires and submitted them to the Lord, he worked things out in my favour and for my good. To this day he has given me almost everything I have asked Him for. I have no doubt that the things that haven't come to pass will come to pass in Jesus name!

I want to give you one last thought. When you begin to put down the desires of your heart, think hard because Jesus gives us a warning.

...From everyone to whom much has been given, much will be required; and to whom they entrusted much, of him they will ask all the more.

Luke 12:48 (AMP)

Jesus is talking about stewardship here. He tells us that as we gain and prosper in life God will require more of us. As we get the desires of our heart we must understand that we must give more back. This can be in the form of more consecration to God or the giving of our wealth and influence to help those with less. I choose to invite people over my house to fellowship with family and friends when God blessed us with a beautiful home. I know some folks that won't even invite their own family over because they will cause wear and tear on their house.

Sometimes people begin to prosper financially and instead of giving more to ministries and charitable organizations, they give less. My faith shot up when God gave me the woman of my dreams. And because of that, I knew that God wanted more obedience from me, so I choose to take ministry more seriously and give God my all. When you ask for more, remember you must give more.

So go ahead and dare to let your heart dream again. What do you really want? The love of your life? The family of your dreams? Maybe you seek love and acceptance from God. Do you want to live in abundance? Do you want to be free from anxiety and depressions? Do you want God to use your life in a powerful way? What is it? Dream and pray. God can help you uncover the things he has placed in you. He can show you what makes you happy. God knows you better than you know yourself. He designed you and placed the desires in your heart...

Before I formed you in the womb I knew you, and before you were born I consecrated (set you apart for me) you...
Jeremiah 1:5 (NIV)

Reflection

Questions for Chapter 16

Answer the following questions taken from this section, and focus your mind

Write down your answers and thoughts

4. Which Step is the easiest to accomplish for you, and why?

_____

_____

_____

_____

_____

_____

_____

_____

_____

_____

_____

5. Which step do you see as the hardest, and why?

_____

_____

_____

_____

_____

_____

_____

_____

_____

_____

_____

_____

6. What is the first, second, and third step you can start taking today to get the desires of your heart?

a_____

_____

b_____

_____

c_____

_____

Chapter 17

Lessons from the Past

The men and women of God were often very prosperous

I was raised in the Church my whole life since I was 7 years old. I belonged to as many as 10 different denominations during this time.

Ironically, my life with my family was lived in poverty from day 1, until I left home at 23 years of age. From what I could gather from the pulpit during those years, the only thing that really mattered in life was to have a great relationship with God.

I am extremely thankful for learning such a powerful truth. Strangely, though, by watching certain other Christians closely, I began to notice that there had to be many benefits to having a great relationship with the Creator of the Universe. However, within my own community, I was seldom, if ever, made aware of what they were.

Whenever I would sow an interest in attending a college, starting a business, or merely just desiring to own material positions of a good quality, I would often be told by well-meaning godly people:

"Go for it but remember: all of those things do not matter if you should lose your relationship with God or when this world comes to an end."

Yes, I understood what they meant; but with the constant repeat of this thought-pattern, I was taught that I should not put a whole lot of effort into being successful in life, because Jesus was coming soon anyways, so why bother.?

Frequently, I would also hear:

"It is better to be poor but to live right, than to be rich and live wrong." This taught me a *"poor person's mentality"*, meaning that I would always struggle to have my basic needs met, and thinking that that was the norm.

I figured that I was better off being poor, not struggling to accumulate good things. Ultimately, this kind of mentality turned into a cop-out for many people around me, including my family. They would "**settle for less**" in many areas of their life. This mentality of "**the poorer you are, the closer you are to God**" was embedded in many faith-based communities.

Eventually I personally began to explore the "**benefits**" that came with a great relationship with God, and I became excited about the scenario of having a **loving Father** rather than an angry God.

However, time and time again, whenever I became excited about the "**benefits**", wanting to explore them, the repeated thought-pattern "**why bother, the world is going to end**" kept interfering.

It wasn't until I left home and began living on my own that I felt free from all the negative pressure from family- and church members that perpetually seemed to always "**settle-for-less**."

As you would have seen from the earlier chapters of this book, I personally would experience the reality of God's abundant blessing over my life.

In addition, I also get to share the hope and faith that is found in the word of God, that we can be free from the bondage that is poverty and dysfunctional environments that we frequently find ourselves in. That is why I chose to write this book... to share.

Do you want to know something very interesting? Do you know that the Bible talks more about finance than it does about Salvation? Yes! The bible teaches that the proper management of our finances and proper stewardship of what God gives us lead to blessings, not only in our homes but also to those around us and even to the nations!

People do not realize that many of the Godly people the Old Testament of the Bible highlights were very prosperous and lived very blessed lives. Whether it was **Abraham that got the child he always wanted** at the old age of 100, or **Moses who led the people out of Egypt** into the desert, or **Joseph who became the administrator** of the food stores of the most powerful nation of the world at the time and was subsequently in the most favorable position to be able to save his entire family... **God always provided *all of* their needs**.

The *Hebrew* people, who were God's chosen people, were extremely well-off (when obedient), even when there was famine in the land. God would perform miracle after miracle to provide for those that trusted Him to the end.

Please note that I am not stating that all Christians have to be rich or have a lot of things; what I am saying is that we don't have to be the poorest either. People do not have to be financially "rich" to be "blessed", we can simply have more than enough to a point where we can freely share with others. I will show you in God's word how prayers full of faith and righteous living lead to many blessings in the Bible that could also be yours!

Abraham

The introductory story of *Abraham* associates wealth with righteous living and puts both as a sign of God's blessing. From the beginning, God made his promise simple and straight forward to the man whom he would use to transform the world, and all because he chose to believe Gods word.

The LORD had said to Abram, "Go from your country, your people and your father's household to the land I will show you.

"I will make you into a great nation, and I will bless you; I will make your name great and you will be a blessing. I will bless those who bless you, and whoever curses you I will curse; and all peoples on earth will be blessed through you.

Genesis 12:1-3 (NIV)

And Abram was very rich in cattle, in silver, and in gold.

Genesis 13:2 (KJV)

Then Abram believed in (affirmed, trusted in, relied on, remained steadfast to) the LORD; and He counted (credited) it to him [a]as righteousness (doing right in regard to God and man).

Genesis 15:6 (AMP)

Undeniably, the verb in the last line of **Genesis 12:2** is actually in the authoritative tense, matching the authority in **verse 1**:

"Go . . . Be a blessing . . . and all peoples on Earth will be blessed through you."

Abraham receives the blessing and becomes the tool to bless others. This is one of the strongest connections where the blessings of God are directly connected to our obedience.

Isaac

The link is even clearer with Isaac.

I will make your descendants as numerous as the stars in the sky and will give them all these lands, and through your offspring all nations on earth will be blessed, because Abraham obeyed me and did everything I required of him, keeping my commands, my decrees and my instructions."

Genesis 26:4-5 (NIV)

Isaac planted crops in that land and the same year reaped a hundredfold, because the LORD blessed him. 13 The man became rich, and his wealth continued to grow until he became very wealthy.

Genesis 26:12-13 (NIV)

Even strangers would have acknowledged God's supernatural blessings over Isaac's house:

That you will do us no harm, just as we did not harm you but always treated you well and sent you away peacefully. And now you are blessed by the LORD

Genesis 26:29 (NIV)

Simply put:

Faith + Obedience = <u>Gods overflowing blessings for not only your home but for others as well.</u>

Boaz

Now Naomi had a relative on her husband's side, a man of great standing from the clan of Elimelech, whose name was Boaz.

Ruth 2:1 (NIV)

The son of *Rahab* and *Salmon*, *Boaz* was a wealthy landowner of *Bethlehem* in *Judea*. He possessed land, servants, good harvests, and the spare cash to redeem *Elimelech's* land. *Boaz's* character emerges throughout the story, which paints *Boaz* as a righteous man.

By saving the land of *Naomi* and taking her and his widowed daughter-in-law, *Ruth*, and raising a son to inherit *Elimelech's* line rather than his own, *Boaz* fulfils the role of <u>kinsman-redeemer</u> and was much-admired by the local community and blessed by God with the birth of his son who would become the ancestor of King David and eventually of Jesus. *Boaz's* generosity stands in contrast to the closer related kinsman who declines to do his duty for the family.

Job

Those of you who need more solid proof that righteous living brings prosperity and physical blessing needs to look no further than Job. He is described an "**upright, blameless and perfect man of God.**"

> *Then the LORD said to Satan, "Have you considered my servant Job? There is no one on earth like him; he is blameless and upright, a man who fears God and shuns evil." Job 1:8 (NIV)*

> *Then the LORD said to Satan, "Have you considered my servant Job? There is no one on earth like him; he is blameless and upright, a man who fears God and shuns evil. And he still maintains his integrity, though you incited me against him to ruin him without any reason." Job 2:3 (NIV)*

The first few chapters make it very clear that God's blessings, favor and prosperity are clearly on *Job* because of his righteous living. Satan himself knows *Job* and points out his wealth to God while he is trying to cause *Job's* fall. Read the following:

224

"Does Job fear God for nothing?" Satan replied. "Have you not put a hedge around him and his household and everything he has? You have blessed the work of his hands, so that his flocks and herds are spread throughout the land.

Job 1:9-10 (NIV)

The test that *Job* is unknowingly exposed to, is to see if his righteousness will survive the loss of all his substance, even his health. While everything is literally stripped away from him, he tells us how he lived his life. We get a deep and insightful view at the life of a righteous man. A generous and loving man that gave back to those with less.

Remember the framework entitled *"pop quizzes"* that I provided in **Chapter 16**? I had mentioned that sometimes the tests would require us to give back. *Job* is the "poster child" of a generous and giving person. What's more interesting, is that he was not a political leader or even part of the lineage of Jesus. *Job* was just a normal, godly person who used his influence and power to help those with less. *Job*, in his moral apologia continues to give us more insight into his integrity:

"If I have denied the desires of the poor or let the eyes of the widow grow weary, if I have kept my bread to myself not sharing it with the fatherless but from my youth I reared them as a father would, and from my birth I guided the widow if I have seen anyone perishing for lack of clothing, or the needy without

garments, and their hearts did not bless me for
warming them with the fleece from my sheep

Job 31:16-20 (NIV)

Jobs security was never on his wealth or prosperity. He never gained it through corruptions or questionable ethical dealings, he says:

"If I have put my trust in gold or said to pure gold,
'You are my security,' if I have rejoiced over my great
wealth, the fortune my hands had gained"

Job 31:24-25 (NIV)

God would eventually not only give *Job* back everything that was taken away from him during his test but would double it!

After Job had prayed for his friends, the LORD restored
his fortunes and gave him twice as much as he had
before. All his brothers and sisters and everyone who
had known him before came and ate with him in his
house. They comforted and consoled him over all the
trouble the LORD had brought on him, and each one
gave him a piece of silver[a] and a gold ring.

The LORD blessed the latter part of Job's life more
than the former part. He had fourteen thousand
sheep, six thousand camels, a thousand yoke of oxen
and a thousand donkeys. And he also had seven sons
and three daughters. The first daughter he named

Jemimah, the second Keziah and the third Keren-Happuch. 15 Nowhere in all the land were there found women as beautiful as Job's daughters, and their father granted them an inheritance along with their brothers.

After this, Job lived a hundred and forty years; he saw his children and their children to the fourth generation. 17 And so Job died, an old man and full of years.

Job 42:10-17 (NIV)

Wow, now that's what I am talking about! This whole book can be summed up with the life of *Job*.

Wisdom

Proverbs. The book of *Proverbs* is a gold mine for the theme of the *"righteous rich"*, because so many of its sayings relate to the use (or abuse) of material goods in one way or another.

An early note, consistent with the running thread through the whole book, is that the only acceptable wealth is that which accompanies trust in God, commitment to him, and acknowledgement of him (*Prov. 3:5-10*).

The fear of the Lord is the beginning (or first principle) of wisdom and also the first requirement for "righteous riches". However, though wealth is a positive good in **Proverbs**, it is not the only or the greatest good by any means. Far more important is wisdom—the wisdom that comes from God:

> *Choose my instruction instead of silver, knowledge rather than choice gold, for wisdom is more precious than rubies, and nothing you desire can compare with her.*
>
> *Prov. 8:10-11, cf. 16:16 (NIV)*

As we saw, *Solomon* knew this in his humbler youth (**1 Kings 3**) but sadly forgot it rather quickly.

The upright also recognize that wealth is in any case no protection against death (***Prov. 11:4***), a relativizing perception that is amplified in even more melancholy tones in ***Ecclesiastes 5:13-6:6***.

The dominant note in relation to *"**righteous riches**"* in **Proverbs**, however, is one that is completely consistent with the law and the prophets, namely the requirement to treat the poor with kindness and without contempt, mockery, or callousness.

Interestingly, however, whereas the law and prophets ground such teaching in the history of Israel's redemption (specifically in God's saving generosity in the Exodus), the **Wisdom** tradition tends to appeal to the broader foundation of creation.

Inconsistencies of human wealth are ultimately irrelevant to our standing before God. Rich and poor are equal before God. Consequently, whatever attitude or action the rich adopt toward the poor, they actually adopt toward God (with all that it entails).

The "**righteous rich**" are therefore those who see their God when they look at the poor man made in God's image:

> "*He who oppresses the poor shows contempt for their Maker, / but whoever is kind to the needy honours God*"
>
> *Prov. 14:31*

This is a note that can be heard echoing through the following texts:

Proverbs 17:5; 19:17; 22:2, 22; 29:7, 13.

As we saw in *Psalm 37*, the **Wisdom Writers** cared more about justice than about prosperity, a perspective which they summarized in the opinion that it was far preferable to be poor but righteous than to have ill-gotten wealth through injustice and oppression. (*Prov. 16:8; 28:6*).

One final perspective worth mentioning is the value of "*contentment with sufficiency.*"

Neither excessive poverty nor excessive wealth are desirable, for both are a temptation to behave in ways that disown or dishonor God. The implication seems to be that the "*righteous rich*" know when to say, "*Enough is enough*":

> *Give me neither poverty nor riches,*
> *but give me only my daily bread.*
> *Otherwise, I may have too much and disown you*
> *and say, "Who is the LORD?"*
> *Or I may become poor and steal,*
> *and so dishonor the name of my God.*

(Prov. 30:8-9)

Wisdom

If I were able to give just **one** piece of advice in our quest for a greater and more fulfilling life, I would advise you to acquire **Wisdom** as fast and absorbent as possible.

The Bible contains the greatest book by far ever written on **Wisdom**: it is the **Proverbs** written by **King Solomon**.

The book of Proverbs is a *"**golden goose**"* ready to lay *"**eggs of righteous wisdom**"* that will prepare you for riches beyond your wildest dreams, because so many of its sayings relate to the use (and sometimes abuse) of material goods in one way or another. **Proverbs** is consistent with its message throughout the whole book. The message is simple: *that the only acceptable wealth is that which comes with trust in God and commitment to him.*

Trust in the LORD with all your heart and lean not on your own understanding; in all your ways submit to him, and he will make your paths straight. Do not be wise in your own eyes; fear the LORD and shun evil.

This will bring health to your body and nourishment to your bones. Honor the LORD with your wealth, with the first fruits of all your crops; then your barns will be filled to overflowing, and your vats will brim over with new wine.

Proverbs 3:5-10 (NIV)

Fear (reverence) + Wisdom from God = <u>righteous riches/a good life</u>

"<u>True Wisdom comes only from God</u>"

Choose my instruction instead of silver, knowledge rather than choice gold,

for wisdom is more precious than rubies, and nothing you desire can compare with her.

Proverbs 8:10-11 (NIV)

"<u>True Wisdom is better than winning the lottery</u>"

How much better it is to get wisdom than gold! And to get understanding is to be chosen above silver.

Proverbs 16:16 (NIV)

We must also take notice that a warning companies the book of Proverbs. This warning is there to remind us that when we start drifting into our own *"stupidity"* or pride then we choose not to listen to Gods word.

*The wise store up knowledge, but the mouth of a fool
invites ruin.*

Proverbs 10:14 (NIV)

King Solomon, who wrote most of the book of
Proverbs, knew these wise words early in his life and
applied them, but sadly, he quickly forgot them later in
his life. Moreover, because of that, he ended up making
many mistakes and committed greats sins before God.

*As Solomon grew old, his wives turned his heart after
other gods, and his heart was not fully devoted to the
LORD his God, as the heart of David his father had
been.*

1 Kings 11:4 (NIV)

I would like to point out something very powerful:
Simply because you acquire wealth and health, and
prosper materially, that does not mean it will bring you
happiness or a fulfilled life. Many people simply use
God as a means to their end-goal without developing a
personal, honest and transparent relationship with
God. That is an inadequate use of God's promises. The
2nd book of wisdom in the Bible, **Ecclesiastes**, warns us
of this potential downfall very clearly.

*I have seen a grievous evil under the sun: wealth
hoarded to the harm of its owners, or wealth lost
through some misfortune so that when they have
children there is nothing left for them to inherit.*

232

Everyone comes naked from their mother's womb, and as everyone comes, so they depart. They take nothing from their toil that they can carry in their hands. This too is a grievous evil: As everyone comes, so they depart, and what do they gain, since they toil for the wind? All their days they eat in darkness, with great frustration, affliction, and anger. This is what I have observed to be good: that it is appropriate for a person to eat, to drink and to find satisfaction in their toilsome labor under the sun during the few days of life God has given them—for this is their lot. Moreover, when God gives someone wealth and possessions, and the ability to enjoy them, to accept their lot and be happy in their toil—this is a gift of God. 20 They seldom reflect on the days of their life, because God keeps them occupied with gladness of heart.

6 I have seen another evil under the sun, and it weighs heavily on mankind: 2 God gives some people wealth, possessions and honor, so that they lack nothing their hearts desire, but God does not grant them the ability to enjoy them, and strangers enjoy them instead. This is meaningless, a grievous evil. A man may have a hundred children and live many years; yet no matter how long he lives, if he cannot enjoy his prosperity and does not receive proper burial, I say that a stillborn child is better off than he. 4 It comes without meaning, it departs in darkness, and in darkness its name is shrouded. 5 Though it never saw the sun or knew anything, it has more rest than does that man— 6 even if he lives a thousand years twice over but fails to enjoy his prosperity. Do not all go to the same place?

Ecclesiastes 5:13-6:6 (NIV)

Wealth and prosperity is not the end game here; it's simply a blessing that God wants us to have, and He can give it to us **here** and **now**.

Wisdom appeals to the larger groundwork for creation. Inconsistencies of wealth are ultimately irrelevant to our standing before God. The rich and poor have a "created equality" as human beings before God.

Whatever approach or action the rich adopt toward the poor, they are really adopting it toward God. The "righteous well-off" are then those who see God when they look at the poor man made in God's image:

Whoever oppresses the poor shows contempt for their Maker, but whoever is kind to the needy honors God.

Proverbs 14:31 (NIV)

I have a mentor that is a missionary, and the last thing he has on his mind is money. Yet God has used him and provided for him in amazing ways to enable him to spread the gospel all over the world. I do understand that there are certain people that feel they do not want more than enough. Perhaps they feel that they cannot trust themselves with an abundance of material wealth, or perhaps they don't want to be burdened with the responsibility that comes with it. To those people I say:

"It's just fine. In fact, the Bible even refers to those that think this way."

Keep falsehood and lies far from me; give me neither poverty nor riches, but give me only my daily bread. Otherwise, I may have too much and disown you and say, 'Who is the LORD?' Or I may become poor and steal, and so dishonor the name of my God.

Proverbs 30:8-9 (NIV)

The prayer of Jabez

When it comes to crazy faith-based prayers that challenge us all, no one does it better than the prayer of **Jabez**. There have been countless of books written on this strange man and his simple and powerful prayer.

The bible doesn't say much about him. In fact, he only has 2 verses that ever mention his name.

His prayer truly shows us not only a huge level of faith, but it also gives us an amazing look into the heart and mind of God.

Often we think of faith as some sort of thing that we all have but the Bible makes it clear that some have or choose to develop a faith that few are willing to live out. This faith makes living a Christian life super exciting and extremely worth the difficult process that it sometimes can be. As you read this prayer, ask yourself these questions:

- *What kind of man was Jabez?*
- *Why does Jabez feel entitled or deserving of such a request?*
- *What does his prayer tell us about his relationship with God?*
- *Why does God not chastise him for what can be seen by many as a prideful and arrogant prayer?*
- *Why does God give him exactly what he wants?*

Once you are able to answer these questions, you will have a new insight into the heart and mind of God! Here is His prayer, and God's response:

Jabez was more honorable than his brothers. His mother had named him Jabez,[c] saying, "I gave birth to him in pain." Jabez cried out to the God of Israel, "Oh, that you would bless me and enlarge my territory! Let your hand be with me, and keep me from harm so that I will be free from pain." And God granted his request.

1 Chronicles 4:9-10 (NIV)

I don't know about you, but is this not the most radical and life-changing prayer you have ever heard? I know I never had heard of it in Sunday school, much less in the adult services at the churches that I attended.

What a faith, what a relationship Jabez must have had with God. I truly believe that when we are able to boldly make this prayer our own personal prayer, only then will God show and give us amazing things!

I can go on and on writing down many more examples that not only will challenge you but also take your prayers and faith to another level. I have dedicated this chapter to all of those who have never been told about the promises that God has for us here in this world.

There are **5,467 promises in the entire Bible**. How many of them do you know, and how many of them are waiting to be plucked out and received?

I challenge you to attend Bible studies, watch YouTube videos and learn more about God's love and promises to his people.

In the blockbuster hit movie, **The Matrix**, *Neo* was given the choice to either take the blue pill that would end the story and return him to the life as he had lived and believed, or the red pill which would keep him in *Wonderland* and he would be shown how deep the rabbit hole goes.

You now stand at a crossroads. You may either choose to believe God's promises or choose not to. And like Morpheus said:

*"Remember: all I'm offering is **the truth**.*

Nothing more

Reflection

Questions for Chapter 17

Answer the following questions taken from this section, and focus your mind

Write down your answers and thoughts

Write out your contract with God, then pray it out... and then hold tight for the ride of your life! Trust Trust Trust!

_____

_____

_____

_____

_____

_____

_____

_____

_____

_____

_____

_____

_____

_____

_____

Epilogue

I want to sincerely tell you that you are **very special** to God and that you are **not an accident**.

God truly wants to give you the desires of your heart.

Let me tell you, all you have to do is take one small step at a time. God will meet you there, which in turn will raise your faith a bit more.

Then you take the next small step, God will meet you there, and your faith again will rise.

Do you see? **Take it *one step at a time*.**

Maybe your first step is as simple as talking to God for the first time. Maybe your next step is getting involved in your local church? And after that, conquering your marriage and finances, or even starting a business...

God will meet you there.

But without faith, it is impossible to please Him, for he who comes to God must believe that He is and that He is a rewarder of those who diligently seek Him.

Hebrews 11:6 (NKJV)

Take Care

Jesus Loves You

Victor Armando Martinez

Victor Armando Martinez

Made in the USA
Lexington, KY
25 May 2018